THE
FILIPINO
INSTANT POT
COOKBOOK

THE FILIPINO INSTANT POT COOKBOOK

Classic and Modern Filipino Recipes
for Your Electric Pressure Cooker

Tisha Gonda Domingo
Jorell Domingo
Jeannie E. Celestial
Art Swenson
Romeo Roque-Nido
Jaymar Cabebe

Photography by Nancy Cho

Rocketships &
Wonderment

Design by Dianne Que and Art Swenson
Edited by Jaymar Cabebe
Translations by Dianne Que

Printed in the United States of America
First Printing, 2019
ISBN 978-1-7341241-0-1

Rocketships & Wonderment
www.rocketshipsandwonderment.com

To Naomi, Bruno, B'jani, K'layaan, MJ, and Mars
The world is your kaldero.

introduction

BAYANIHAN | THE SPIRIT OF COMMUNITY

After borrowing her mom's Instant Pot and letting it sit on the kitchen counter for months, Tisha and her husband Jorell finally decided to give it a try with a recipe for honey garlic short ribs. The end result was rich with garlicky goodness and buttery soft meat that was basically dripping off the bone. It was so yummy that Tisha and Jorell became instant Instant Pot addicts. They searched for recipes online, scouring Facebook for groups of other IP home cooks. They found a few nice Instant Pot communities, but were ultimately disappointed that none of them were sharing much Filipino food. So, they decided to create a new Facebook group: Filipino Recipes Instant Pot Community. It first picked up steam among friends of friends, then, seemingly in lockstep with Amazon's growing IP sales, the group blew up by the thousands. Suddenly, from their home in Southern California, Tisha and Jorell found themselves connecting Filipino food fanatics from around the world.

Meanwhile, about 400 miles away, in Northern California, Jeannie, Art, Romeo, and Jaymar had been throwing around the idea of writing a Filipino cookbook for busy parents. Naturally, recipes for the Instant Pot came to mind. They were excited to share their versions of Filipino flavors with other families who might enjoy them. And real talk, they wanted to join in on the rapid growth of Filipino food in mainstream American culture.

Through mutual friends, the six of us connected. We all had similar values and motivations—healthy home-cooked meals, time-efficient and budget-friendly recipes, and a strong connection to Filipino culture, especially the food. But what really made us feel like kindred spirits was our sense of responsibility to explore the culinary traditions of our motherland, to connect more deeply with our parents and grandparents, and to preserve our heritage by passing it on to our children (and eventually grandchildren). This was really the force that drove us to work together on this book.

ABOUT US

We are all second-generation Filipina and Filipino Americans, born to parents who immigrated here from the Philippines in the '60s and '70s. Jeannie and Jorell were born on Guam, while the rest of us were born in California. While we may not be professional chefs or food historians, the six of us are certainly well-practiced (and always learning) home cooks who have a profound love for the Filipino foods we grew up with. At the same time, we all have growing families (together, we have six kids under the age of eight!) with practical constraints that make cooking quick homemade meals critical to our daily lives. The Instant Pot electric pressure cooker is, of course, our collective weapon of choice.

ABOUT THE BOOK

The recipes in this book were compiled from family, personal friends, and many, many recommendations. In our writing, we tried to maintain some type of consistency across the recipes, but it was also important to us that we preserve the voice of each individual author. After all, we each have unique stories and styles that inform our cooking (and writing). That said, there are basic elements you can expect for every recipe in the book:

- Serving Size or Yield
- Estimated Prep Time
- Estimated Active Time (Example: Sauté time when you have to be attentive to your pot)
- Pressure Cook Time (This does not include the time it takes for the IP to come to pressure, as that can vary based on many factors.)
- Release Type (Natural Pressure Release vs. Quick Release)

Additionally, you can be sure all recipes have been tested and iterated on multiple times with our 6-quart Instant Pots (most of us have the Duo). The bulk of the work involved translating inexact stovetop family recipes into more precise Instant Pot-friendly versions. It wasn't always easy, but it was always fun!

Lastly, a word about authenticity. The Philippines is a nation of over 7,600 islands and almost 200 languages, so it's no wonder there's so much variation across Filipino cooking methods, dishes, and ingredients. That's why your lola's arroz caldo might not match someone else's, even though both could probably be considered "authentic" depending on who's eating. In this book, we try to offer a mix of more popular variations of dishes along with some lesser-known favorite renditions.

So, dive in and have fun preparing true Filipino comfort food. Explore our Filipino roots with us, and enjoy the stories and dishes coming straight from the hearts of our families and into the bellies of yours.

Maligayang pagdating sa mundo ng paglulutong Instant Pot!

Tisha & Jorell
Jeannie & Art
Romeo
Jaymar

TISHA GONDA DOMINGO
Philippines Home Province: Romblon & Batangas
US Hometown: Orange County, CA
Favorite Recipes: Tinolang Manok (page 62) and Leche Flan (page 134)

JORELL DOMINGO
Philippines Home Province: Parañaque & Cavite
US Hometown: Los Angeles, CA via Sagamihara, Japan
Favorite Recipes: Mechadong Baka (page 94), Nilagang Baka (page 92), and Leche Flan (page 134)

JEANNIE E. CELESTIAL
Philippines Home Province: Cebu & Cavite
US Hometown: Vallejo, CA
Favorite Recipes: Nut-Free Kare-Kare (page 101) and Mango Royale Cheesecake (page 150)

ART SWENSON
Philippines Home Province: Pampanga
US Hometown: Oakland, CA
Favorite Recipes: Dinuguan (page 77) and Hamonadong Baboy (page 85)

ROMEO ROQUE-NIDO
Philippines Home Province: Nueva Ecija
US Hometown: Vallejo, CA
Favorite Recipes: Sardinas na Bangus (page 115) and Ginataang Sitaw at Kalabasa (page 129)

JAYMAR CABEBE
Philippines Home Province: Samar, Pangasinan, & Ilocos Sur
US Hometown: Diamond Bar, CA
Favorite Recipes: Arroz Caldo (page 46) and Ginisang Upo (page 122)

CHAPTER 1

instant filipino food

I was four years old in Tondo, Manila, Philippines. It was morning. Two of my uncles were holding a goat when someone else (don't remember who) came by and gently put a bottle of vinegar in its mouth. To this day, I don't know what it was for, but apparently it was important. Everything seemed like it was happening really fast. Then, all of a sudden, the goat was down. And, like choreography, everyone instantly shifted to different roles, cleaning and prepping the animal.

Later that afternoon, I could see and smell smoke burning in the alley. What really impressed me was that this was all happening in one day.

Since then, I've been fascinated with cooking—the different phases of it, the teamwork aspect, and the refusal to waste any ingredients. Growing up in California, I enjoyed watching my lola cut, chop, boil, fry, grill, and bake for hours. She lived with us, and I would spend entire days in the kitchen with her, asking questions.

Today, as a busy father and partner, I still maintain the same sense of fascination with food, albeit under different circumstances. My lola has passed, and my parents don't live with us. I don't have a bunch of relatives at the house to help me go from farm to table by mid-afternoon. The reality is that after commuting, picking up the kids, and doing my other fatherly duties, there isn't much time left to cook dinner. That's where our little Instant Pot shines. It helps me get homemade sinigang on the table in 45 minutes instead of two hours. And my family is grateful for it.

With the IP, we feel fortunate that we don't have to eat an uncomfortable number of frozen or fast casual meals per week. We can have homemade Filipino food on a daily basis if we like. And that's a comfort we, through our recipes and stories in this book, hope to share with you.

-Romeo

A HISS-TORY OF PRESSURE COOKING

Pressure cooking certainly didn't find its way into Filipino cuisine because of the Instant Pot. The method has, in fact, been employed by Filipino home cooks and chefs for decades, as it was rumored to have been brought to the Philippines when the country was colonized by the United States over a century ago. The older stovetop version of the pressure cooker, however, was considered by many to be intimidating with its clunky inter-locking lid and perceived safety issues. Still, it managed to find its way into the kitchens of many of our lolos and lolas.

So, why is it that pressure cooking makes so much sense for Filipino cuisine? If we take a look at the methods used in most of our dishes, it's easy to see the answer.

If you quickly go through all your memories of Filipino home-cooking in your head, you'll probably realize that the oven makes very few appearances relative to the stove. That's because the most common Filipino dishes call for "moist-heat" cooking methods. That is, their ingredients are braised, simmered, or boiled in water and other natural juic-es, often for long periods of time. Think about nilaga, sinigang, bistek, adobo, and many of your other favorites. These dishes are some of the most popular in our culture, and they all call for proteins (beef, fish, pork, chicken, and so on) to be broken down and tender-ized, always with moisture. And the resulting soups and stews are served hot alongside a bed of warm steamed rice (also cooked with moist heat). As it turns out, these are exactly the types of dishes that pressure cookers were designed for.

INSTANT OBSESSION

The pressure cooker is having a cultural moment. Consider this: many of today's families experience a work-life imbalance that makes cooking at home difficult; yet, there has been a documented rise in families opting to eat in. With this in mind, it's clear that today's home cooks are the perfect market for an appliance that can simplify and speed up meal prep.

The Instant Pot brand is taking advantage of this. It does programmable pressure cooking well, plus it includes conveniences that past generations' cooks could only dream of. On top of all that, there's just something about the brand that resonates with busy home cooks—Filipino or otherwise.

It's important to note that all of the Instant Pot models have a base set of features that is good enough to cook the recipes in this book. But there are a few differences that might make you consider going for a higher-end model. On the following page is an overview of Instant Pot's current lineup.

- *Lux* - This is the baseline model with six different pressure programs. While it's a perfectly good appliance, it's less popular because it lacks the low-pressure mode that can be useful for more delicate foods like eggs and some vegetables or fish.

- *Duo* - Instant Pot's most popular model, the Duo is a step up from the Lux with its seven programs, including one for yogurt. It also includes two different pressure settings—low and high—which add versatility without breaking the bank.

- *Ultra* - With the Ultra, you're in the big leagues, as this model includes all the functionality of its less feature-packed siblings, plus it allows you to cook at specific temperatures, instead of just the HP and LP options. Additionally, it gives you an updated self-closing pressure valve.

- *Max* - The Max is a significant step up from the other models for many reasons, but its biggest draws are its higher max pressure and much improved temperature sensors. Because of this added precision, the Max model includes a sous vide function that lets you cook in an accurately regulated water bath.

- *Smart* - Finally, if you're willing to shell out the extra bucks, the Smart WiFi model offers most of the features of its siblings, plus it hooks up to a mobile app and gives you the ability to download recipes, program complex cooking steps, and share it all with friends.

At the end of the day, regardless of which model you choose, we think the most important consideration should be the size of your Instant Pot. As mentioned, all of the different models offer the functionality to cook the recipes in this book, so your first order of business should be targeting one that's appropriately sized for your family. Most models come in 3-quart, 6-quart, and 8-quart sizes. The 6-quart is the most popular size, so a good idea would be to start there and decide whether to scale up or down.

Lastly, with the simplicity and versatility of the Instant Pot, many "power users" tend to own more than one, and we don't think that's such a bad idea. For instance, if you like to play handaan host, running two IPs can significantly cut your prep time. And if you're short on shelf space, you could even get a mini IP, which is great for sides and smaller individual meals.

CORE FLAVORS

Filipino cooking is made up of intense core flavors that are intended to pair with the mildness of plain white rice, making for a delicious balance of opposites. In many dishes, we get heavy sour tones from vinegar, citrus fruits, or tamarind, that are then followed closely by the fermented aromas, umami, and saltiness of soy sauce, patis, and bagoong. The body of the flavors comes from the meat, fat, and aromatics like onions, garlic, bay leaves, and ginger. And finally, fun accents like tomato, chilies, bell pepper, bitter melon, and coconut milk round out the tail end of every bite, and linger on the tongue.

Our most potent flavorings tend to come in bottles or jars and embrace fermentation. Think vinegar, soy sauce, patis, and bagoong—all made by fermenting various ingredients, allowing microorganisms to metabolize them, to alter their composition and enhance their flavor. Fermented foods are quite common even in American staples like beer, cheese, sourdough, and yogurt. But Filipino fermentation goes further toward the extremes of sourness, fishiness, and funkiness, such that sniffing a bottle of vinegar or patis qualifies as a small act of bravery. Yet, when used in savory dishes, these powerful potions yield uniquely delicious results.

Most Filipinos are meat-lovers at heart, requiring at least one form of animal protein to pair with rice per meal. This is where the sour flavorings come in. Adding a fair amount of vinegar or citrus juices to meats, especially offals like liver and tripe, cuts through the richness and can really make a dish taste notably Pinoy. It's the sour notes in our recipes that always make our mouths water. Consider sisig (calamansi), sinigang (tamarind), bistek (lemon), and adobo (vinegar). Yum.

When salting our dishes, we rarely use simple table salt alone. Most commonly, we turn to fermented soy sauce and patis to add both saltiness and umami flavor at the same time, reserving salt for the fine-tuning of flavors when necessary. In fact, you could name basically any savory Filipino dish, and each one probably has some amount of soy sauce, patis, or both.

As for aromatics, Spanish influence gave us the gift of onions and garlic, which we usually sauté first, to get our savory dishes started. Other aromatics such as ginger, bay leaves, chilies, tomatoes, or bell peppers are common in the sauté too, but can also be added later to the pot as it simmers, depending on the needs of the dish.

Ultimately, what we want is for you to think about the roles the ingredients play when cooking Filipino recipes, so that you can improvise with flavors on your own. Take a basic adobo recipe with its main ingredients being white vinegar (sourness), soy sauce (saltiness and umami), chicken (meat and fat), garlic, onions, and bay leaves (aromatics). If you wanted to add some complexity, you could try sneaking in some supplemental ingredients that fall within the major flavor roles. For example, you might add a pinch of sinigang mix to make the sour flavor more interesting. Perhaps you'd drop in a tablespoon of patis to add depth to the umami. You could try using wings and thighs for more tenderness and fat, or just throw in some pork belly. And maybe add a thai chili to your aromatics for heat, and some coconut cream to make the gravy richer. By adding these supplemental ingredients, you've just turned plain-Jane adobo into the adobo sa gata recipe featured in this book!

UNDER PRESSURE

You may remember from science class that water boils at exactly 212-degrees Fahrenheit. In the kitchen, this is important because if you heat your food any higher than that, the water in your dish will vaporize, often leaving behind tough, moisture-depleted ingredients. Of course, what this means is that there is a very clear limit on the degree of moist heat you can use when you're cooking.

But what if we could actually raise cooking temperatures beyond this limit without jeopardizing the texture or taste of our food? Pressure cooking allows us to do just this and with great results. By trapping water and steam in a tightly sealed pot (pressure cooker), we can cook foods at higher temperatures while retaining all the moisture and natural flavors our ingredients need to maintain optimum yumminess. The elevated pressure inside the pot also serves to quickly tenderize meats, so, as a result, cooking times are cut significantly. For many, the pressure cooker is an indispensable appliance.

More than just a pot with an air-tight lid, the Instant Pot is a fully electric pressure cooker for the modern-day cook, with added features like a delayed start timer, automatic release valve, and even WiFi connectivity on some models. And most importantly it comes with a multitude of different cooking modes (more on those later).

As you start your culinary exploration, it's important to first get to know a few terms that will help you understand Instant Pot recipes.

HIGH PRESSURE MODE (HP) When set to HP, the Instant Pot can reach an internal pressure range of 10.2 to 11.6 psi (pounds-per-square-inch), bringing cooking temperatures to a maximum of 240 degrees. Meanwhile, the Instant Pot Max model can go even higher and hotter, achieving up to 15 psi and 250 degrees.

LOW PRESSURE MODE (LP) When set to LP, the Instant Pot's internal pressure ranges from 5.8 to 7.2 psi, bringing cooking temperatures to a maximum of approximately 230 degrees.

NATURAL PRESSURE RELEASE (NR OR NPR) When a pressure-cooking program completes, the Instant Pot automatically begins to slowly release air and steam from its release valve, preventing liquids from spraying out of the pot and ingredients from moving inside. Natural pressure release is ideal for foods with high liquid volume or starch content and low risk of overcooking.

QUICK PRESSURE RELEASE (QR OR QPR) Quick Pressure Release is used to quickly stop the cooking process to prevent overcooking. Different from NPR, however, this can result in some agitation inside the pot and venting steam from the release valve. This is ideal for quick-cooking vegetables or other delicate foods like seafood.

Regional Variations

Filipinos around the world are known for displaying fervent pride, not just for their country, but also for their home region. See, the Philippines has three main island groups—Luzon, Visayas, and Mindanao—which together contain 17 distinct regions. Interestingly, these regions often espouse their own versions of traditional Filipino dishes, altering flavors based on the history, subcultures, and geography that are specific to those areas.

Take adobo, the unofficial national dish of the Philippines. The indigenous process of marinating fish or meat in vinegar was universally used to preserve foods in the tropical climate long before Spanish colonization. So, this dish has an enduring history across the archipelago. A basic recipe calls for protein, vinegar, garlic, soy sauce, and peppercorns, but so many elements can vary widely between regions and even between families. The vinegar-to-soy sauce ratio can swing from one side of the spectrum to the other. Some people prefer their adobo saucy; others, dry. Bicolanos of Southern Luzon add coconut milk and chilies to their adobo sa gata (page 59). Batangueños omit soy sauce and use luyang dilaw (turmeric) to create a yellow, gingery adobo (page 60). In coastal regions, Filipinos enjoy adobo made with seafoods, such as adobong pusit (squid) and adobong hipon sa gata (shrimp adobo in coconut milk). Flavors can vary even further, with some people including sugar, onion, achuete (annatto seeds), and laurel (bay leaves).

Growing up, I couldn't get enough of my mom's chicken adobo with lots of sabaw (sauce) to pour over rice and fresh laurel from her garden, which infused each bite with a floral aroma. Meanwhile, Dad's adobong pula (red adobo) was also great but very different. Bright orangey-red with achuete and loaded with roughly cut garlic, Dad's adobo hearkened back to his Luzon roots.

Regardless of region and regardless of dish, the most consistent ingredient we can include in our cooking is love. Imagine the intention and care our nanays, lolas, and other family members put into all of their dishes. Without question, it's love that enhances the flavors, forging the food we now crave over and over.

-Jeannie

filipino pantry

Looking into a proper Filipino pantry doesn't just give you an idea of our country's native tropical ingredients. Rather, it offers you a window into its storied past—from ancient Indo-Malaysian migration and trade with neighbors around Asia, to a centuries-long occupation by the Spanish empire and an oft-forgotten war with the United States. The culinary profile of the Philippines in some ways, offers a lesson on colonialism and cultural evolution.

Still, with its melting pot of non-indigenous influences, Filipino food has managed to forge its own identity, with distinct flavors and common ingredients found across many of its dishes. Here, we'll do our best to highlight some of these.

Also, while we do strive to use homemade ingredients when possible, there are some cases where using ready-made flavor packets is almost unavoidable. For instance, with sinigang, fresh sampalok (tamarind)—the original souring agent used—can be hard to come by, so we use sinigang powder, which, now is so widely used that it has come to be regarded by many as an "authentic" ingredient anyway.

AROMATICS

As a home cook, you may have noticed that most savory recipes are built on a foundation of aromatics—that is, a combination of herbs, spices, and/or vegetables cooked in a fat, like oil or butter. In this book, you'll see that Filipino recipes tend to follow suit, with the Filipino aromatic base typically consisting of onions and garlic... lots and lots of garlic. With this in mind, stocking your pantry with these aromatic staples is a must, as you get started.

Olive Oil or Vegetable Oil
Because of health benefits like monounsaturated "good" fats and antioxidants, we tend to default to olive oil. However, it does have a lower smoke point than other oils, so it may not be the best option for recipes that require very high heat to do things like sear or fry. For these, we'll typically use vegetable oil. That said, other oils can be used based on your preference (coconut oil, anyone?).

Onions
Onions are the basis of many dishes. Typically we add them first to hot oil, at which point, they develop their sweetness and coloring depending on the level of heat exposure. Yellow onions are most commonly used, but can usually be substituted with white onions.

Garlic

You can never put too much garlic in a Filipino dish. With this in mind, it's best to keep your pantry stocked with a few heads at a time. Common fresh white garlic usually does the trick. Pre-peeled is fine, but in most cases, we would advise against the pre-minced variety that comes preserved in oil, as it can dramatically alter your dish's flavor.

Ginger

Commonly included in Filipino soups, ginger can be used grated, finely chopped, or thinly sliced. The tough flesh of the root isn't always meant to be eaten directly, but instead is used simply as a flavoring agent. Look for pungent ginger with thin skin that can easily be scraped off with your nail. That's how you know it's fresh.

Dried Bay Leaves

Sharp and bitter, dried bay leaves are often used in hearty Filipino stews like menudo, mechado, and adobo. Like ginger, however, these leaves aren't usually eaten, but instead used as a flavoring agent then removed or set aside.

SPICES & SEASONINGS

With the many variations of dishes in Philippine cuisine, it would be tough for us to identify all of the spices and seasonings you'd ever need in your pantry. Instead, we're highlighting some of the most prevalent, so you can at least cover the staples.

Salt

Salt is perhaps the most important item in your pantry. Like many home cooks, we like Diamond Crystal brand Kosher salt. It's less salty and more flaky, which means you can get better coverage and more consistent flavoring without over-salting.

Black Pepper

For the dishes in this book, we recommend keeping both whole peppercorns and ground pepper on hand. And of course, using a fresh grinder is always best.

Annatto Powder

Brought to the Philippines from Mexico on a Spanish galleon, annatto is a spice derived from the achiote tree. It has a mildly sweet and sometimes peppery flavor, but is mostly used as a food coloring. If you can't find it in your local chain grocer, try stores that specialize in Latin American or Asian foods.

Garlic Powder

Sometimes a recipe calls for dried, ground, and pulverized garlic. Don't confuse this ingredient, garlic powder, with garlic salt, which is a mixture of ground garlic and salt.

Turmeric Powder

Look for the organic variety to maximize turmeric's many health benefits. And be sure to cook with turmeric spice, which is different from the popular health supplement.

Paprika

We tend to default to regular or "sweet" paprika. The Hungarian variety offers a bit more spice, while smoked paprika gives off a, you guessed it, smoky flavor. These other kinds are certainly usable, but may change the flavor of your dish.

Sugar

Many of our recipes use light brown sugar. But if you like the deep flavor of molasses, you can try experimenting with dark brown or even muscovado sugar, which is less processed. For white sugar, default to the granulated variety used in cooking and baking.

CONDIMENTS & OTHER ESSENTIALS

To finish off your pantry, consider a handful of other Filipino "essentials" to keep in light stock. You'll find that they're needed in multiple recipes, either as key ingredients for cooking or condiments to enjoy with your dish.

Patis (Fish Sauce)

If salt is the most important ingredient in the pantry, patis is a close second. Its savory, umami flavor adds a uniquely Filipino quality to many dishes, so when it's missing you definitely know it. Some recipes call for patis as a seasoning during cooking, while others benefit from it as sawsawan (dipping sauce) at the dinner table. While just about every country in East and Southeast Asia has its own version of fish sauce, we tend to stick with Filipino brands like Rufina or Datu Puti.

Bagoong (Shrimp Paste)

When we mention bagoong, we're usually referring to the pink-colored paste, bagoong alamang, which is made of fermented shrimp. However, there's also a reddish brown version, bagoong isda, that substitutes the shrimp for fish, and offers an interesting alternative. To get the most out of your adventures in Philippine cooking, try both. And of course, don't forget about bagoong guisado aka ginisang bagoong, the lightly sautéed version of the shrimp paste that is widely used as a condiment. You can buy it pre-made or prepare it yourself by sautéing with garlic, onions, and other ingredients.

Coconut Milk

Fresh gata (coconut milk) can be hard to find, and it spoils very quickly, so we stock the canned variety, which works just fine. Also, we prefer the slightly more expensive organic brands, which have fewer additives. For stronger coconut flavor, you can try using coconut cream, which is concentrated and has a thicker consistency.

Rice

Of course, kanin is absolutely essential to any Filipino meal, so stock up before working your way through this book. White tends to be more popular than brown, as it absorbs the flavors of soups and stews more easily (though it lacks some of the health benefits of brown). With your meal, most rice varieties will work, so ultimately the choice is yours.

Soy sauce

There are seemingly innumerable brands of toyo (soy sauce) to suit your preferences. As a basic cooking ingredient, we again have a bias for Filipino brands like Silver Swan or Datu Puti. Kikkoman is another favorite, which offers a lower sodium option that still creates great flavoring.

Calamansi

While this Philippine fruit used to be quite difficult to find, calamansi has grown in popularity, so you can get it in many specialty supermarkets today. For our purposes, it's best to opt for the fresh fruit, rather than any extract or juice, as the peel itself is also a valuable ingredient.

White Vinegar

Filipinos love the asim (sour) quality in food, and vinegar is often the key to developing it. Skip the crystal-clear distilled varieties and opt for the typically cloudier Filipino favorites like Datu Puti's Sukang Maasim. We consider this particular bottle a good default choice for its milder flavor. Meanwhile, other vinegars offer varying levels of acidity to suit your palate.

Spiced White Vinegar

Also known as sukang maanghang, this variety isn't used much in cooking. Rather, this tangy pinoy vinegar adds chilies, garlic, and other ingredients to create what many consider the perfect sawsawan (dipping condiment). Since you'll be enjoying lots of Filipino food over the course of this book, we highly recommend stocking a few bottles.

Apple Cider Vinegar

It's not as universally used in Filipino cooking as white vinegar, but many recipes do call for ACV, as it helps to add a bit of complexity and sweetness to sour dishes. We like the raw, unfiltered variety.

ESSENTIAL EQUIPMENT

Undoubtedly, what sets the Instant Pot apart from other pressure cookers is its versatility. Not only does the appliance offer an assortment of different cooking modes—from sauté to slow cook to yogurt—but it also takes advantage of an ever-growing number of accessories designed to level up your cooking and make your life a bit easier. Here, we'll go over a few Instant Pot-specific accessories, as well as some other crucial cooking tools to have in your kitchen as you start cooking these Filipino favorites.

Tempered Glass Lid

Sitting atop our recommendation list is the tempered glass lid for the Instant Pot. This must-have accessory gives you both coverage (no splattering!) and visibility while you're using non-pressure-cook modes like Sauté, Slow Cook, and Keep Warm. Even better, you can use the lid to easily store food in the refrigerator, saving you from having to transfer between containers.

Take a look at the genuine glass lid offered by Instant Pot, as it's sure to fit perfectly, is oven and dishwasher safe, and offers the same warranty as your appliance.

Extra Inner Pot

Coming in a close second to the glass lid, is another must-have, the extra inner pot. Take a moment to consider all the different functions of your Instant Pot. Now, can't you imagine a day will come when you'll want to prepare an entire multi-dish meal in your pressure cooker? Maybe an ulam (main dish) and a veggie side to serve together? Or an even more basic pairing like chicken adobo and rice? With the extra inner pot, you can pull the first dish out and get started on the second without delay.

Again, the genuine Instant Pot option works best here, as you're guaranteed compatibility and quality. Also, IP offers both original stainless steel and nonstick varieties.

Silicone Lid

While the tempered glass lid can be used for food storage, its drawback is that it doesn't create an airtight or watertight seal over your food. The flat silicone lid gives you this benefit in an easy-to-store, dishwasher-safe option. It's perfect if you have multiple inner pots in rotation. And again, Instant Pot offers a genuine accessory that's relatively inexpensive.

Steamer Rack Trivet

Some recipes call for the "pot in pot" method, where a smaller cooking vessel like a pot or bowl is placed directly inside your Instant Pot. Think cheesecake or pot pie. For recipes like these, it's important to use a steaming rack, as it helps to elevate the vessel off the floor of your inner pot and out of your cooking liquid. Most Instant Pot models come with a handled steamer rack trivet that should more than suffice. But if you want to stock another, you can try a steamer set that comes with stackable steaming vessels. Having one of these sets offers the convenience of steaming a few different foods in one go.

Springform Pan

If sweets are your bag, you'll be excited to know that the Instant Pot is also adept at cooking desserts (see Minatamis chapter, page 133). But of course, for some of these sweets, you'll need a springform pan that fits snugly into your Instant Pot. There is no shortage of options designed specifically for use inside the Instant Pot, but make sure to get the right size based on your model (7 to 7½-inches in diameter for 6qt IP). Also, try using parchment liner in your pan to prevent sticking.

One thing to note, if your pan doesn't have handles, is that you may need to get creative when removing it from your inner pot. A popular option is the "foil sling," or a long strip of aluminum foil wrapped around the underside of your pan, with edges long enough to serve as handles. It's a simple trick that can be used whenever you're cooking with the pot-in-pot method.

Steamer Basket

Different from steamer racks and pans, a steamer basket is a bit more versatile. It's not a necessity, but you can use it to hold vegetables or other loose ingredients that need to be kept out of the cooking liquid for steaming. Additionally, you can use it as an in-pot colander to hold bones or vegetables while you boil a stock. For extra convenience, try one with a folding handle.

Wooden Spatula or Spoon

Because many of our recipes call for a short sauté step before moving on to pressure cooking, it's nice to have a non-metal utensil to mix your ingredients as they sizzle. For best results, try a flat-ended wooden spatula, which should help with scraping those flavorful browned bits that can get stuck to the bottom of your pot.

Of course, there's a whole debate about wooden cooking utensils versus plastic or silicone. We won't get into any of that here, but we will say that while we've modernized our cooking appliance, there's something comforting about sticking with the same wooden tools our lolos and lolas used as they prepared these same dishes.

Ladle

A lot of the dishes we'll explore in this book are brimming with sabaw, so make sure you've got a nice long ladle for serving and stirring. A total length of seven inches or more will help you reach the bottom of the pot.

Tongs

Make sure you have a nice pair of tongs to reach the bottom of the deep inner pot. This will make it easier to not only remove foods, but also flip them as you brown with the Sauté function. A twelve-inch pair with silicone or nylon heads will work nicely in both the stainless and non-stick inner pots.

Fat Separator

If you haven't used a fat or gravy separator before, it's essentially a measuring cup that draws or pours liquids out from its bottom up. This allows you to capture all your flavorful juices while leaving fats floating up top. It's not a necessary tool, but it's a nice-to-have if you're turned off by the translucent layer that can sometimes accumulate on the surface of some dishes.

Ay, the Gasket!

Take a stroll through any Instant Pot forum on the Web, and you're sure to find at least a handful of people with questions about the Instant Pot's gasket or sealing ring. It's a critical part of your appliance, as it ensures an airtight pressure seal between lid and pot. But with its flexible silicone composition, it does have some issues.

First, over time, the sealing ring can become less effective as it wears. With normal usage, you shouldn't see this happen for two to three years. But if you really put your pot through its paces, you might need to have some replacements on hand sooner.

Second, is the infamous odor issue. Because it's made of silicone, the ring tends to absorb smells over time, which can cause some transfer of unappetizing flavors. To protect against this, it's important to clean your sealing ring regularly and thoroughly.

For regular cleaning, remove the ring from the lid and place it in the dishwasher. A strong detergent, plus the heat will remove most odors. For deeper cleaning (or if you don't have a dishwasher), try making a cleaning solution with 2 cups of white vinegar and cut-up lemon rind. You can use this solution to run your Instant Pot's steam function (4 minutes should do) or simply soak your ring in overnight. Either method should do the trick.

You might also consider having two rings, one for savory dishes and one for sweet. It's a little more work to swap rings in and out, but it's well worth it if you use your IP frequently for both pungent savory foods and delicate desserts.

frequently asked questions

What Filipino dishes can I make in an Instant Pot?

The IP certainly shines with stews and soups that traditionally require a long simmer, but it's also great for cooking so many other types of dishes. You can use it to tenderize meats before finishing them in the oven or on the grill. You can even use it for pancit. The possibilities are endless!

Where it does fall short, though, is with deep-fried dishes. Sauté mode is great for stir frying, but deep frying is not recommended by the manufacturer. As an alternative, you can make delicious crispy dishes like Lechon Kawali (page 86) by starting with the Instant Pot (for the majority of the cooking) and finishing in the oven or air fryer for maximum crispiness.

How about desserts?

Absolutely! The IP is great for a wide variety of desserts, but especially those that are typically steamed, like leche flan, puto, or kutsinta.

What about dishes that have both meat and veggies? Can I cook those at the same time?

Depending on the dish, you may need to cook the meat first before releasing the pressure and adding in the vegetables. Then, you may or may not have to bring the pressure up again. For instance, potatoes, carrots, and other harder veggies may require additional pressure cooking, while leafy greens like spinach or kangkong won't.

Can I cook rice in the Instant Pot?

The Instant Pot is great for cooking rice, especially brown rice (if you're looking for a healthier option). Measurements may differ slightly from your standard rice cooker.

What do QR and NPR mean?

These terms refer to the different types of pressure release. Some recipes might call for a Quick Release, sometimes noted as QR—where you flip the pressure release valve open immediately after cooking—while other recipes might call for a Natural Pressure Release sometimes noted as NPR or NR—where you just leave the valve as-is so the pressure can slowly release on its own. Depending on what's in your pot, it can take 10-15 minutes or more for the pressure to naturally release. In this book, we'll use the terms Quick and Natural, with a few of the recipes requiring some combination of the two.

Can I really cook a dish in 20 minutes (or whatever time the recipe says)?

Yes. Sort of. Some recipes might say 20 minutes, but what they're referring to is the time under pressure. For example, a pork dish may require 20 minutes under pressure, but you must also take into account the amount of time it takes for that pressure to build up in your pot. This could add five to ten minutes or more, depending on the amount of food inside (liquid and solid), the temperature of the food (frozen meats take longer to come to pressure), and even the altitude of your home. And then, of course, there's the time it takes to release the pressure. So, in actuality, the pork dish above could take 7 minutes to come to pressure, 20 minutes to cook, and 10 more minutes to NPR for a total of 37 minutes, plus your prep time. Regardless, the Instant Pot should still be significantly faster than traditional cooking methods.

For your convenience, the recipes in this book break down prep time, active time (if, for instance, you need to actively stir and sauté), and pressure cook time to give you a better idea of how long it will actually take to cook a dish.

My kitchen was a mess after I cooked a dish and tried quick-releasing the pressure. What happened?

Cooking some dishes, especially soups or stews that fill your pot, can sometimes cause excess liquid to spray from the pressure release valve when you do a QR. If this happens, you can turn the venting knob with a spoon just enough to allow the steam to release very gradually. You can also try letting the pressure release naturally, but keep in mind, the dish will continue to cook, so you may need to reduce your time under pressure to avoid overcooking.

Why am I getting a BURN notice?

The Burn indicator typically flashes when there's not enough liquid in your dish. To avoid this, you can try adding more water (or other liquid) and keep meats and noodles/pasta from sitting at the bottom of the pot.

Is it possible to overfill the pot?

If you are cooking foods that expand, like beans, pastas, or grains, your pot should not be more than ½ full when you close the lid. And regardless of what you are cooking, it should never be more than ⅔ full.

CHAPTER 2

kanin at pancit
RICE & NOODLES

PANCIT PALABOK
Rice Noodles with Golden Sauce

Serves 6
Prep Time: 20 minutes
Active Time: 10 minutes
Pressure Cook Time: 15 minutes
Release: Natural + Quick

Noodles:

16 oz bihon (rice stick noodles)

Sauce:

2 tbsp cooking oil
1 medium onion, finely chopped
2 tbsp garlic, minced
1 Cornish game hen
1 tsp salt
5 cups broth (chicken, shrimp, or pork broth)
4 tbsp butter (or bacon grease)
1 tbsp annatto powder
¾ cup cornstarch
2 tbsp cold water
½ tsp ground black pepper

Toppings:

2 boiled eggs, diced
½ cup chicharon (no attached fat), crushed
1 green onion, thinly sliced
1 bulb garlic, minced and fried (optional)
5 calamansi, halved
Patis

The "P" in palabok stands for *patience* when making palabok the traditional way. My mom would labor for hours concocting hers: boiling broth, preparing the sauce, myriad toppings, and noodles. The typical sauce is made with shrimp, but my mom has always used chicken as her base. My mother-in-law's palabok recipe is similar except her secret ingredient is Cornish game hen, which happens to be the perfect size for the Instant Pot! Game hens also debone more easily than regular chicken, and the meat is more tender and delicate. Both of my moms approve of this palabok recipe, so we hope you do, too. *-Jeannie*

Prepare the noodles:

1. In a large bowl, soak the uncooked (dried) noodles in very warm water. Set aside allowing the noodles to rehydrate. Check occasionally and strain the noodles once they are al dente. (If you are in a rush, you may boil the noodles to the desired texture.)

Prepare the sauce:

2. Preheat the Instant Pot on Sauté setting. When the inner pot is hot, pour in the cooking oil. When the oil is shimmering, add onion and sweat until translucent. Add garlic and sauté until fragrant.

3. Add game hen, salt, and broth. Select Manual and program for 15 minutes on High Pressure. When cooking is complete, allow pressure to release naturally for 10 minutes and then quick release remaining pressure

4. Unlock and carefully remove the lid. Carefully remove game hen using tongs and place on a medium-sized platter. Remove any fallen bones from the broth. Select Keep Warm and turn and lock the lid into place.

5. Allow hen to cool until safe to touch. Debone hen, discarding bones. Dice the hen meat and set aside.

recipe continues >

PANCIT PALABOK
*Rice Noodles with
Golden Sauce*

continued >

6. In a small bowl, melt butter in the microwave on high for about 40 seconds. Mix the annatto powder into the melted butter until completely dissolved (no clumps).

7. In another small bowl, add cornstarch and 2 tbsp cold water, stirring well to create a smooth slurry.

8. Unlock and carefully remove the lid and select Sauté setting. Bring the broth to a medium boil and slowly add the annatto butter mixture.

9. Add the cornstarch mixture a little at a time, stirring constantly with a whisk until thoroughly incorporated. Allow to boil until the sauce coats the back of a spoon.

10. Gently stir in half of the game hen meat. The remaining half can be served as a topping or used for another dish, such as Lugaw (page 45).

Prepare the fried garlic:

11. In a small skillet over medium-low heat, add 1 tbsp of cooking oil. Add the garlic and sauté until golden, being careful not to burn them. Place in a small bowl and set aside.

Prepare the toppings:

12. Place boiled eggs, chicharon, green onion, fried garlic, calamansi, and patis into separate small serving bowls.

Plate a serving:

13. Fill a bowl or plate with plain noodles. Ladle on sauce. Add toppings as desired. Sprinkle with calamansi and patis to taste.

PANCIT CANTON
Filipino-Style Chow Mein

Serves 4 to 6
Prep Time: 15 minutes
Active Time: 25 minutes
Pressure Cook Time: n/a
Release: n/a

½ lb of boneless,skinless chicken thighs (cut into bite-size pieces)

½ lb prawns, peeled

2 tbsp olive oil

8 cloves garlic, minced

2 medium shallots, chopped

2 Chinese sausages, sliced into ¼-inch discs

½ lb prawns, peeled

1 tbsp ground black pepper

2 cups low sodium chicken broth

4 tbsp low sodium soy sauce

2 tbsp toasted sesame oil

1 large carrot, julienned

¼ of purple cabbage, shredded

16 oz of pancit canton noodles

2 green onions, chopped

2 lemons, quartered (divided)

Salt and pepper to taste

As a kid, I only had pancit at family parties. During my teens, I worked at my uncle's food cart, where we sold it three times a week. For over a decade, during the two-week county fair, we served pancit everyday. I'd even come home smelling like it. Once home, I'd see my lola preparing pancit for the next day. She was the machine behind the food cart and the county fair. Her pancit was delicious. My uncle no longer has the food cart. We're not at the county fair anymore. My lola is no longer around. And I'm back to having pancit only during parties. But these days, I'm the one bringing it. *-Romeo*

1. Season chicken and prawns with salt and pepper

2. Preheat the Instant Pot on Sauté setting. When the inner pot is hot, pour in the cooking oil. When the oil is shimmering, add the garlic and shallots. Sweat until aromatic and soft, about 4 minutes.

3. Add chicken and Chinese sausage to pot, stirring constantly until chicken has browned. Remove the chicken and sausage and set aside.

4. Add prawns to pot, stirring constantly until they are pink and firm. Remove from pot and set aside.

5. Add black pepper, broth, soy sauce, and sesame oil to deglaze pot, scraping any bits that have stuck to the bottom.

6. Place carrots, cabbage, and noodles into the pot. Mix to ensure all noodles absorb liquid. Once noodles have absorbed the liquid, select Keep Warm.

7. Return chicken, sausage, and shrimp to pot. Mix to distribute contents, and turn off Instant Pot. Add salt and pepper to taste.

8. Empty pancit into a serving dish, top with green onions and juice of ½ lemon. Place remaining lemon in a bowl, and serve alongside pancit.

PINOY SPAGHETTI
Filipino-Style Spaghetti

Serves 4
Prep Time: 15 minutes
Active Time: 5 minutes
Pressure Cook Time: 10 minutes
Release: Quick

---

2 tbsp olive oil

1 small onion, diced

½ lb. ground beef

1 cup water

4 hot dogs, sliced (optional)

½ tsp dried oregano

½ tsp dried parsley

¼ tsp onion powder

¼ tsp garlic powder

½ tsp salt

½ tsp ground black pepper

12 oz. spaghetti noodles

1 to 2 tbsp olive oil

24 oz. tomato sauce

½ cup banana ketchup
(page 156)

¼ cup cheddar cheese, finely
shredded (optional)

Filipino spaghetti evokes childhood memories of my aunt's sunny kitchen in San Francisco. Auntie Julita made the best spaghetti—chunky noodles coated with a savory, sweet sauce and tiny morsels of beef and hot dogs, laced with melted U.S. government cheddar cheese. You'll feel good about making this version of Filipino spaghetti for the kids and grown-ups in your life. This recipe uses minimally processed ingredients, red sauce and banana ketchup, essentially from scratch. Serve this pasta on its own or pair it with our Meatball Shanghai (page 103). Hot dogs and cheese are optional. *-Jeannie*

1. Preheat the Instant Pot on Sauté setting. When the inner pot is hot, pour in the cooking oil. When the oil is shimmering, add the onion and sweat until aromatic and soft.

2. Add ground beef and brown thoroughly.

3. Add water and deglaze the pot. Turn off Instant Pot.

4. Add hot dog (optional). Stir in oregano, parsley, onion powder, garlic powder, and salt.

5. In a large bowl, break the noodles in half and massage them with olive oil until coated. Add the noodles to the inner pot arranging them loosely in varying directions.

6. Pour tomato sauce and banana ketchup over the noodles, ensuring they are completely covered.

7. Turn and lock the lid into place, making sure the steam-release valve is in the sealed position. Select Manual and program for 10 minutes on High Pressure. When cooking is complete, quick release pressure manually.

8. Serve and sprinkle with cheddar cheese as desired.

KAYUMANGGING KANIN

Brown Rice

Serves 4 to 5
Prep Time: 2 minutes
Active Time: 0 minutes
Pressure Cook Time: 15 minutes
Release: Natural

---

2 cups long-grain brown
   rice, rinsed

2½ cups water

1 tbsp butter

Bread, eggs, sugar, and rice—kitchen staples that I grew up knowing only as white. I'm not sure if it was due to availability or just a cultural norm. Today, if these items are in our house, they're brown. We started eating brown rice as a healthier alternative. Compared to white, it isn't as sticky, and it tastes more like a grain than starch. Brown rice's longer cooking time makes it a good candidate for the Instant Pot. Compared to the white rice experience of my teen years, I'm glad brown rice doesn't require me to carry a 50-pound bag from car to house then pour its contents into a 3-foot tall rice dispenser. *-Romeo*

1. Add rice, water, and butter to the inner pot.

2. Turn and lock the lid into place, making sure the steam-release valve is in the sealed position. Select Manual and program for 15 minutes on High Pressure. When cooking is complete, allow pressure to release naturally.

3. Stir and fluff rice before transferring to a serving bowl.

BRINGHE NI LOLA

Grandma's Native Paella

Serves 4
Prep Time: 5 minutes
Active Time: 16 minutes
Pressure Cook Time: 12 minutes
Release: Quick

---

3 tbsp cooking oil

4 boneless chicken thighs, cut into 2-inch strips

½ green bell pepper, sliced into ½-inch strips

½ red bell pepper, sliced into ½-inch strips

1 (2-inch piece) ginger, minced

2 bay leaves

4 tbsp patis, divided

5 cloves garlic, crushed

1 medium onion, minced

3 chicken livers, cut into ½-inch slices

2½ tsp turmeric powder

1½ tsp ground black pepper

4 cups coconut milk

Patis, salt, and pepper to taste

3 cups glutinous rice, rinsed

Lola, I miss you. You were a powerhouse of great cooking, and your bringhe in particular brought down the house. It was the decadent, savory, and sticky masterpiece you dubbed "yellow rice." When I asked you what the secret of your bringhe's flavor was at the séance, the psychic medium replied in your voice, "Cook the rice in pure coconut milk." Okay, that didn't actually happen, but... I do believe you would approve of my Instant Pot interpretation of your recipe. -*Art*

1. Preheat the Instant Pot on Sauté setting. When the inner pot is hot, pour in the cooking oil. When the oil is shimmering, add chicken thighs, red and green bell peppers, ginger, bay leaves, and 2 tbsp patis. Sauté mixture until chicken is browned.

2. Add garlic, onions, chicken liver, turmeric powder, and pepper. Sweat until the onions are translucent and the liver becomes firm, about 3 minutes.

3. Add coconut milk. Adjust seasoning to be slightly salty with remaining patis, salt, and pepper.

4. Add glutinous rice and stir until combined. Select Manual and program for 12 minutes on Low Pressure. When cooking is complete, quick release pressure manually.

5. Unlock and carefully remove the lid. Select Slow Cook and leave uncovered for 10 minutes. Adjust seasoning with salt.

TIP:

Add that 'just-like-Lola' touch to your bringhe with a crispy crust. Bake the finished bringhe in a baking pan lined with banana leaves at 350 degrees for 20 minutes, or until your desired crispiness.

ARROZ VALENCIANA
Filipino-Style Paella

Serves 5 to 6
Prep Time: 10 minutes
Active Time: 20 minutes
Pressure Cook Time: 7 minutes
Release: Quick

---

2 tbsp cooking oil

2 tbsp butter

1 medium onion, diced

½ lb boneless skinless chicken thighs, cut into bite-sized pieces

1 head of garlic, minced

1 tbsp smoked paprika

1 tbsp turmeric

1 tsp ground black pepper

2 tsp salt

2 cups bomba rice

3 cups low sodium chicken broth

2 Spanish chorizo sausages, cut into 1-inch thick slices

2 pinches saffron threads

½ lb large prawns, peeled and deveined

4 oz package frozen green peas

1 red bell pepper, cut into strips

My lola used to make Arroz Valenciana for birthday parties and special occasions. I wasn't a fan of the sticky, slightly sweet rice she used. This recipe replaces the malagkit rice with bomba rice (aka Valencia rice). I've learned that the dish is derived from Spanish paella. If you want to add some sweetness to this dish, use Chinese-style sausage instead of chorizo. This dish is great for potlucks. It's easy to cook, full of flavor, and very colorful. *-Romeo*

1. Preheat the Instant Pot on Sauté setting. When the inner pot is hot, pour in the cooking oil. When the oil is shimmering, add butter and onions and sauté until onions are soft.

2. Add chicken, garlic, smoked paprika, turmeric, black pepper, and salt, stirring until chicken is browned.

3. Add rice and stir well. Add broth, chorizo, and saffron, scraping up any bits stuck to the pot.

4. Turn and lock the lid into place, making sure the steam-release valve is in the sealed position. Select Manual and program for 7 minutes on High Pressure. When cooking is complete, quick release pressure manually.

5. Unlock and carefully remove the lid. Add prawns, peas, and bell pepper and select Sauté. Stir until prawns are cooked through and liquid is completely absorbed.

CHAPTER 3

lugaw at sabaw

PORRIDGE & SOUPS

left, Sotanghon, page 47

LUGAW
Plain Rice Porridge

Serves 8
Prep Time: 10 minutes
Active Time: 5 minutes
Pressure Cook Time: 15 minutes
Release: Natural

---

2 tbsp cooking oil
1 tbsp garlic, minced
½ cup onion, finely chopped
1 (1-inch piece) ginger, thinly sliced
1 cup rice (glutinous or other), rinsed
8 cups water
Patis and black pepper to taste

Toppings (optional):

Scallions or chives, chopped
Deep-fried tofu
Crushed chicharon
Raw egg yolk
Lemon or calamansi juice
Fried dilis or danggit
Honeycomb beef tripe (see "goto" version)

Growing up, my grandparents' kitchen table was always stocked with essential items: a jar of instant coffee, sugar, small bottles of patis and toyo, and various snacks. There often was a small pot of lugaw, ready for consumption at any time of the day. Lugaw is the plainest form of Filipino porridge, usually made with leftover rice that can be flavored with toppings of your choice. As a kid, I enjoyed adding one raw egg yolk with a couple pinches of salt to my lugaw for a quick merienda. Lugaw is easy on a queasy stomach, commonly used to nurse a cold or flu. *-Jeannie*

1. Preheat the Instant Pot on Sauté setting. When the inner pot is hot, pour in the cooking oil. When the oil is shimmering, add the garlic, onion, and ginger and sweat until aromatic and soft. Turn off Instant Pot.

2. Add rice and water, stirring until combined. Turn and lock the lid into place, making sure the steam-release valve is in the sealed position. Select Porridge Mode and program for 15 minutes on High Pressure. When cooking is complete, release pressure naturally.

3. Unlock and carefully remove the lid. Serve and add toppings as desired. Adjust seasoning with patis and black pepper.

Make the goto (optional):

1. Prepare tripe for goto before making the lugaw. Wash ½ to 1-pound of tripe and place in the inner pot.

2. Add 1 tbsp white vinegar, 1 tbsp lemon juice, 1 tbsp salt, and enough water to fully cover tripe.

3. Cook on Manual Setting for 20 minutes on High Pressure. Quick release when cooking is complete.

4. Remove tripe, let cool, and cut into ¼ to ½-inch pieces. Add to cooked lugaw as desired.

ARROZ CALDO
Chicken Rice Porridge

Serves 4
Prep Time: 5 minutes
Active Time: 15 minutes
Pressure Cook Time: 20 minutes
Release: Natural + Quick

---

4 chicken thighs, skin removed
Salt and pepper
3 tbsp cooking oil, divided
5 cloves of garlic, minced
½ medium white onion, diced
1 tbsp grated ginger
3 cups water
3 cups low sodium chicken broth
3 tbsp patis
1 cup rice, long grain or
    short grain

Toppings:
1 bulb fried garlic
    (page 34)
2 lemons, quartered
1 green onion, thinly sliced
Crushed chicharon (pork rinds)

As a kid, my mom would feed me a steaming hot bowl of arroz caldo every time I was sick with a cold or flu. I didn't believe in its healing powers, but it did feel good when I'd go to the stove for a second or third helping. As an adult, I appreciate this thick and creamy porridge for its rich flavor. Tender chicken is balanced with the perfect mix of toppings: crunchy fried garlic and tangy calamansi juice. And, of course, now I serve this to my family when they're sick. -*Romeo*

1. Pat the chicken dry with a paper towel and season with salt and pepper. Set aside.

2. Preheat the Instant Pot on Sauté setting. When the inner pot is hot, pour in 2 tbsp of cooking oil. When the oil is shimmering, add the garlic, onion, and ginger and sweat until aromatic and soft, about 2 minutes.

3. Add chicken thighs. Cook for 2 minutes on each side.

4. Add broth, water, and patis. Stir and scrape the bits that have stuck to the bottom of the pot. Add rice and stir until combined.

5. Turn and lock the lid into place, making sure the steam-release valve is in the sealed position. Select Manual and program for 20 minutes on High Pressure.

6. When pressure cooking is complete, allow pressure to release naturally for 10 minutes, then quick release.

7. Ladle the porridge into bowls and top with green onions and fresh black pepper. Serve with lemon, patis, and fried garlic on the side.

SOTANGHON
Mung Bean Noodle Soup

Serves 4 to 6
Prep Time: 15 minutes
Active Time: 20 minutes
Pressure Cook Time: 15 minutes
Release: Quick

---

3 tbsp cooking oil

4 cloves garlic, minced

1 small yellow onion, chopped

1 lb skinless, bone-in
   chicken thighs

4 tbsp patis

3 cups water

½ tsp annatto powder

4 cups chicken broth

1 carrot, julienned

4 oz sotanghon

2 cups Napa cabbage or
   cabbage, shredded

Salt and pepper to taste

Toppings (optional):

4 hard-boiled eggs, sliced

Green onion, thinly sliced

1 bulb fried garlic (page 34)

It has been tradition for my mom to make sotanghon on New Year's Eve, and I always look forward to eating it to mark the end of another year. Sotanghon is our version of chicken noodle soup consisting of mung bean thread noodles, shredded chicken, and vegetables. It's cooked in an aromatic broth with onion and garlic, and the annatto powder (achuete) gives the broth the bright yellow color. To top it off, I like to add sliced hard-boiled eggs, chopped green onion, and crunchy fried garlic to my bowl of sotanghon. *-Tisha*

1. Preheat the Instant Pot on Sauté setting. When the inner pot is hot, pour in the cooking oil. When the oil is shimmering, add the garlic and onion, and sweat until the onions are translucent.

2. Add chicken thighs and patis. Lightly brown chicken and mix until patis evaporates, about 6 to 8 minutes.

3. Add water to pot. Turn and lock the lid into place, making sure the steam-release valve is in the sealed position. Select Manual and program for 15 minutes on High Pressure.

4. When cooking is complete, quick release pressure manually. Unlock and carefully remove the lid. Remove chicken and place on a plate to cool.

5. In a small bowl, mix annatto powder and ½ cup of hot broth from the pot, stirring until dissolved.

6. To remove chicken from bones, shred chicken using 2 forks or by hand.

7. Select Sauté and add chicken broth, shredded chicken, and annatto mixture.

8. When broth is boiling, add carrots and cook for 2 minutes. Add sotanghon and cabbage and cook for 2 minutes.

9. Adjust seasoning with salt and pepper. Ladle soup into bowls and top with desired toppings.

MISUA AT BABOY
Thin Wheat Noodles and Pork

Serves 4
Prep Time: 10 minutes
Active Time: 5 minutes
Pressure Cook Time: 5 minutes
Release: Quick

½ lb ground pork

2 tbsp patis

½ tsp ground black pepper

2 tbsp cooking oil

1 tbsp garlic, minced

½ cup chopped onion

2 tbsp finely minced ginger

4 cups broth (chicken, pork, or shrimp)

1 medium patola, peeled and cut into ½-inch discs

½ lb shrimp

2 to 4 oz of misua noodles

Patis and black pepper to taste

Misua always reminds me of my dad. It was one of the dishes he would make when Mom was too busy to cook. This dish was probably in Dad's rotation because it's fairly simple to make and involves fresh vegetables, which he loved. Patola is also known as ridge sponge gourd or Chinese okra. Misua is a very thin vermicelli made of wheat flour. In this light soup, the aromatics combine with chunks of ground pork, delicate shrimp, and the earthy flavor of the patola. The misua ties it all together, starchy and comforting. *-Jeannie*

Prepare the pork:

1. In a medium-sized bowl, combine the pork, patis, and black pepper. Set aside to marinate.

Prepare the soup:

2. Preheat the Instant Pot on Sauté setting. When the inner pot is hot, add cooking oil. When the oil is shimmering, add garlic, onion, and ginger and sweat until aromatic and soft.

3. Push the aromatics to one side of the inner pot to clear the cooking surface. Place the ground pork in the pot and flatten, forming one big "burger." Cook the pork until browned then break the "burger" into bite-sized chunks.

4. Turn off Instant Pot. Add the broth and deglaze the pot. Then, add patola and shrimp, stirring until combined.

5. Turn and lock the lid into place, making sure the steam-release valve is in the sealed position. Select Manual and program for 5 minutes on High Pressure. When cooking is complete, quick release pressure manually.

6. Unlock and carefully remove the lid. Add the misua, which will soften immediately into the hot soup.

7. Adjust seasoning with patis and black pepper to taste.

SOPAS
Creamy Chicken Macaroni Soup

Serves 6
Prep Time: 15 minutes
Active Time: 15 minutes
Pressure Cook Time: 7 minutes
Release: Quick

---

3 tbsp cooking oil

4 cloves garlic, minced

1 large yellow onion, chopped

3 medium carrots, diced

2 celery stalks, diced

6 cups chicken broth

1 lb boneless skinless
   chicken thighs

2 cups elbow macaroni

1 (12 oz) can evaporated milk

Salt and pepper to taste

Surprisingly, I only discovered this dish about 10 years ago when I was visiting my soon-to-be in-laws in Seattle. It looked so simple, but I found it to be so comforting and delicious; I remember going back for a second and a third bowl. Variations of this dish call for sliced hot dogs, ham, cabbage, corn, or hard-boiled eggs, so feel free to make this recipe your own. *-Tisha*

1. Preheat the Instant Pot on Sauté setting. When the inner pot is hot, pour in the cooking oil.

2. When the oil is shimmering, add garlic, onion, carrots, and celery and cook until onions are translucent, about 5 minutes.

3. Add chicken broth and chicken thighs.

4. Turn and lock the lid into place, making sure the steam-release valve is in the sealed position. Select Manual and program for 7 minutes on High Pressure. When cooking is complete, quick release the pressure manually.

5. Unlock and carefully remove the lid. Remove chicken thighs and shred chicken. Set aside.

6. Select Sauté setting and bring the soup to a boil. Add elbow macaroni and cook for 10 minutes or until pasta is cooked.

7. Add shredded chicken, evaporated milk and stir. Adjust seasoning with salt and pepper.

TIP:

Feel free to substitute whole or low-fat milk for evaporated milk.

PANCIT MOLO
Pork Dumpling Soup

Serves 4 to 6
Prep Time: 45 minutes
Active Time: 30 minutes
Pressure Cook Time: 10 minutes
Release: Quick

---

3 tbsp cooking oil

4 cloves garlic, minced

¼ cup yellow onion, chopped

½ lb skinless bone-in
   chicken thighs

2 tsp salt, divided

1½ tsp ground black
   pepper, divided

2 bay leaves

8 cups water

2 tbsp patis

Salt and pepper to taste

1 lb ground pork

1 small carrot, shredded

⅓ cup green onions, chopped

2 cloves garlic, minced

¼ cup water chestnuts, chopped

1 egg

1 tsp sesame oil

1 package of wonton wrappers
   (approximately 50 wrappers)

Toppings (optional):
Green onions, chopped
1 bulb fried garlic (page 34)

Pancit molo, or pork dumpling soup, was a dish my mom used to make for me all the time when I was younger. It was also a huge hit with my friends. This particular recipe is a bit more labor intensive because it involves making dumplings from scratch. But the results are completely worth the effort. And for my fellow garlic lovers, don't forget to garnish the soup with fried garlic—it's a definite must! I love to meal prep, so this recipe makes double the dumplings so you can freeze the extras. That way they're ready to cook the next time you crave pancit molo. -*Tisha*

Make the soup:

1. Preheat the Instant Pot on Sauté setting. When the inner pot is hot, pour in the cooking oil. When the oil is shimmering, add the garlic and onion cooking until onions are translucent.

2. Add chicken thighs and brown both sides. If necessary, you can add 1 to 2 tbsp oil to prevent chicken from sticking to pot. Add 1 tsp salt, 1 tsp pepper, bay leaves, and water to the pot.

3. Turn and lock the lid into place, making sure the steam-release valve is in the sealed position. Select Manual and program for 10 minutes on High Pressure. When cooking is complete, quick release pressure manually. Remove chicken and set aside.

Make the dumplings:

4. In a large bowl, combine ground pork, carrot, green onions, 2 cloves minced garlic, water chestnuts, egg, sesame oil, 1 tsp salt, and $\frac{1}{2}$ tsp pepper, and mix well.

recipe continues >

PANCIT MOLO

Pork Dumpling Soup

continued >

5. Separate a wonton wrapper and place on a plate. Scoop approximately 1 tbsp of mixture into the middle of the wrapper. Dip your finger in a small bowl of water and wet the edges of the wonton wrapper. Fold the wonton to form a triangle and press the sides down pushing out any air bubbles around the filling. Set aside on a plate. Repeat until all the meat mixture has been used.

6. To cook the dumplings, select Sauté setting on Instant Pot and bring the soup to a boil. Add about 20 to 25 dumplings to the soup and cook for 5 to 6 minutes. Dumplings will float to the top once they are done cooking. (Note: Freeze the remaining dumplings in a freezer bag and lay flat in freezer so dumplings don't stick together.)

7. While dumplings are cooking, shred the chicken.

Finish:

8. Add shredded chicken and patis to the soup. Adjust seasoning with salt and pepper.

9. To serve, garnish with fried garlic and green onions.

TIPS:

If you want to add vegetables to the soup, feel free to do so after the dumplings are cooked. Consider adding chopped bok choy, spinach, or napa cabbage and gently boil for 1 to 2 minutes.

If you like shrimp, you can also add chopped shrimp to the dumpling mixture.

To save time, you can use a food processor to finely chop garlic, onions, carrots, and chestnuts.

If you want to simplify this recipe and skip making the broth, you can use pre-cooked shredded chicken and replace 4 cups of water with chicken broth.

CHAMPORADO
Chocolate Rice Porridge

Serves 4 to 6
Prep Time: 2 minutes
Active Time: 5 minutes
Pressure Cook Time: 12 minutes
Release: Natural

---

1 cup sweet rice, rinsed

3 cups water

3 tbsp cocoa mix

1 cup milk

1¼ cup dark chocolate chips

Toppings (optional):
Dilis
Tuyo
Bacon
Sweetened condensed milk
Milk

The first time I encountered champorado was during breakfast at my auntie's house. She ladled some into a bowl and said, "try this chocolate rice," before topping it with dilis (dried and salted anchovies). I passed on the champorado, choosing the Spam and eggs instead. Some folks love the salty and sweet combination of breakfast foods, like a maple bacon donut or a McGriddle. The flavor pairing finally made sense to me when I had a chocolate chip cookie topped with salt crystals. While I still find the dilis version outside of my comfort zone, I do sometimes enjoy my champorado with bacon. But my favorite will always be a plain bowl of chocolatey champorado. *-Romeo*

1. Add rice, water, and cocoa mix to the inner pot. Stir until any lumps of cocoa are completely dissolved.

2. Turn and lock the lid into place, making sure the steam-release valve is in the sealed position. Select Rice setting (12 minutes will display). When cooking is complete, allow pressure to release naturally.

3. Unlock and carefully remove the lid. Add milk and chocolate chips. Stir to evenly distribute.

UBE CHAMPORADO
Ube Black Rice Porridge

Serves 4 to 6
Prep Time: 2 minutes
Active Time: 3 minutes
Pressure Cook Time: 30 minutes
Release: Natural

---

1 cup black sticky rice, rinsed
4 cups water, divided
1¼ cup coconut milk, divided
2 tbsp melted butter
2 tsp salt
1 cup ube halaya

Toppings (optional):
Grated fresh coconut
Toasted coconut shreds
Chopped pistachio nuts

Equipment:
Stainless steel bowl (large enough to hold all ingredients, and fit into the inner pot)

Here's an alternate to the better-known chocolate champorado. I call this "Double Purpp" because it incorporates ube (purple yam) and the purple hued pirurutong (black sticky rice). Pirurutong has a slightly nutty taste, which goes well with the sweet, starchy, and earthy ube. Tell everyone you're making champorado for breakfast and surprise them with this colorful treat. *-Romeo*

1. Place black sticky rice in a stainless steel bowl and rinse.

2. Stir in 2 cups water, 1 cup coconut milk, butter, and salt into bowl. Mix well.

3. Pour 2 cups of water into inner pot, place trivet inside, and place stainless steel bowl on top of trivet.

4. Turn and lock the lid into place, making sure the steam-release valve is in the sealed position. Select Manual and program for 30 minutes on High Pressure. When cooking is complete, allow pressure to release naturally.

5. Unlock and carefully remove the lid. Carefully remove the stainless steel bowl from the inner pot. Add ube halaya, and remaining ¼ cup coconut milk. Stir to evenly distribute contents.

Pambata: Baby and Kid Food

I first purchased the Instant Pot while I was pregnant because I knew that it would be useful for our growing family. One reason I wanted to "IP" was to make bone broth and stews to replenish my postpartum body with collagen and minerals to support healing and lactation. Dishes presented in this book, such as nilaga, sinigang, and bulalo were staples for my recovery. In addition, lactogenic ingredients that increase breast milk supply and nutritional density are also in this book including: ginger, garlic, legumes, carrots, dark leafy greens, malunggay, salmon, (grass-fed) beef, (free range organic) chicken, eggs, olive oil, coconut oil, avocado oil, brown rice, and coconut milk.

Empowered with this new culinary device, I also made our baby MJ's first foods with the IP; for example, lugaw and kalabasa (which I mashed or cubed). Whenever my husband and I made ulam for ourselves in the Instant Pot, I would add extra ingredients for our little one: green leafy vegetables, squash, corn, potatoes, etc. When the dish was cooked, I portioned out servings for MJ, stored them in small glass containers, and dated and froze them for future use. MJ was introduced to many of our native flavors early in her life--ginger, garlic, onion, vinegar, and sampalok--which have helped her develop a wide and adventurous palate. We use organic ingredients in our cooking when possible and especially for produce known to have higher pesticide residues (look online for EWG's "The Dirty Dozen"), such as spinach, kale, apples, tomatoes, celery, and potatoes. This cookbook contains recipes which are meant to suit people of all ages in your family, even your little ones. We've also included Nut-Free Kare-Kare for families like ours with nut allergies.

-Jeannie

CHAPTER 4

manok
POULTRY

left, Adobong Manok, page 58

ADOBONG MANOK

Chicken Adobo

Serves 4 to 6
Prep Time: 8 minutes
Active Time: 8 minutes
Pressure Cook Time: 17 minutes
Release: Natural + Quick

---

2 tbsp cooking oil

12 cloves garlic, minced

2 lbs frozen chicken thighs

¾ cup light sodium soy sauce

⅓ cup apple cider vinegar

⅓ cup white vinegar

½ tbsp patis

1 tbsp ground black pepper

4 bay leaves

You're driving home from work with an exact idea of what the evening is going to be like. Time is portioned out for every activity: dinner, play with kids, watch TV, exercise, then get ready for bed. You get home, walk into the kitchen, and realize you forgot to defrost the chicken! It's OK, your evening isn't ruined. This recipe using frozen chicken is useful when you need to stay on schedule. The classic adobo flavors are still infused into the chicken, so you can breathe easy and be guilt-free.
-Romeo

1. Preheat the Instant Pot on Sauté setting. When the inner pot is hot, pour in the cooking oil. When the oil is shimmering, add garlic and sauté until golden.

2. Add chicken, soy sauce, vinegar, patis, pepper, and bay leaves.

3. Turn and lock the lid into place, making sure the steam-release valve is in the sealed position. Select Manual and program for 17 minutes on High Pressure (10 minutes if chicken is thawed). When cooking is complete, allow pressure to release naturally for 5 minutes and then quick release remaining pressure.

4. Remove chicken from Instant Pot, place on a foil-lined sheet pan, and broil (skin side up) until skin is more crisp than tender.

5. Remove bay leaves from sauce, combine chicken and sauce in a serving dish.

ADOBO SA GATA
Coconut Milk Adobo

Serves 3 to 4
Prep Time: 35 minutes
Active Time: 15 minutes
Pressure Cook Time: 5 minutes
Release: Quick

---

3 tbsp cooking oil

2 lb boneless chicken thighs

5 cloves of garlic, crushed

1 red onion, diced

¾ cup + 2 tbsp coconut cream

¼ cup soy sauce

¼ cup vinegar

1 tsp ground black pepper

3 bay leaves

1 thai chili pepper, whole

Salt, coconut cream, and vinegar
  to taste

Call me a snob but I think straight-up adobo is kind of boring. Meat, soy sauce, vinegar, and maybe some grease on top if you're lucky? That's it? I measured my enjoyment of adobo by how fresh and fluffy the white rice was. In my own cooking, I found myself experimenting with ways to make it more interesting: throw in some tomato, a few potatoes, a chili or two, or a big pinch of sinigang powder. Magic happened when I happened to pour in a can of coconut milk, and I finally fell in love! I later discovered this wasn't a new thing at all. I guess I was late to the party again (just like in real life). *-Art*

1. Preheat the Instant Pot on Sauté setting. When the inner pot is hot, pour in the cooking oil. When the oil is shimmering, add the chicken pieces and brown both sides in batches, approximately 5 to 7 minutes per side, being careful not to overcrowd the pot. Set chicken aside.

2. Add garlic, red onion, and additional oil as needed, and scrape any bits that have stuck to the bottom of the pot. Sweat until aromatic, about 2 minutes.

3. Add chicken, coconut cream, soy sauce, vinegar, black pepper, bay leaves, and thai chili pepper. Turn and lock the lid into place, making sure the steam-release valve is in the sealed position. Select Manual and program for 5 minutes on High Pressure. When cooking is complete, quick release pressure manually.

4. Unlock and carefully remove the lid. Adjust seasoning with coconut cream, salt and vinegar and serve with rice.

TIPS:

Reduce the broth to deepen the flavors to your liking. Set Instant Pot to Sauté and leave uncovered for 5 to 12 minutes.

Add depth to the sour profile with other sour ingredients: balsamic vinegar, sinigang powder, lemon, or calamansi.

ADOBONG DILAW

Turmeric Adobo

Serves 4
Prep Time: 5 minutes
Active Time: 35 minutes
Pressure Cook Time: 20 minutes
Release: Natural + Quick

---

2 tbsp cooking oil
12 cloves garlic, minced
2 lbs chicken thighs
1 tbsp salt
1 tbsp turmeric powder
½ cup apple cider vinegar
1 tbsp patis
1 tbsp ground black pepper
4 bay leaves
1 cup low sodium chicken broth

I loved my uncle's adobo, but one day he told us he made a "special" adobo. When he placed the big blue bowl of bright yellow chicken on the table, I didn't know what to expect. My first thought was, "That ain't adobo!" After tasting it, I was pleasantly surprised that it did have hints of the classic version. This recipe replaces the saltiness and umami of soy sauce with the more bitter ginger taste of turmeric. If you want to bring something new into the dinner rotation, or surprise folks at a party, try this out. *-Romeo*

1. Preheat the Instant Pot on Sauté setting. When the inner pot is hot, pour in the cooking oil. When the oil is shimmering, add garlic and sauté until golden.

2. Add chicken, salt, turmeric, vinegar, patis, pepper, bay leaves, and chicken broth.

3. Turn and lock the lid into place, making sure the steam-release valve is in the sealed position. Select Manual and program for 20 minutes on High Pressure. When cooking is complete allow pressure to release naturally for 10 minutes and then quick release remaining pressure.

4. Remove bay leaves before serving.

PININYAHANG MANOK
Pineapple Chicken

Serves 6
Prep Time: 15 minutes
Active Time: 20 minutes
Pressure Cook Time: 10 minutes
Release: Quick

---

3 tbsp cooking oil

3 lbs bone-in chicken thighs

4 cloves garlic, minced

1 yellow onion, sliced

2 tbsp patis

1 cup pineapple juice

1 cup pineapple chunks

1 large potato, cut into
 1½-inch pieces

1 red or green bell pepper, cut
 into 1-inch pieces

2 medium carrots, cut into
 1-inch pieces

½ cup evaporated milk

Salt and pepper to taste

The Philippines is one of the largest producers of pineapples in the world. So it's no surprise to come across a dish where pineapple is one of the key ingredients. This is one of the few Filipino dishes I know that doesn't use tomatoes or soy sauce for the base. Instead, it is cooked in pineapple juice and finished off with evaporated milk, giving the dish a sweet, creamy, tangy flavor. The pineapple chunks are always a nice surprise when I take a bite of this dish. *-Tisha*

1. Preheat the Instant Pot on Sauté setting. When the inner pot is hot, pour in the cooking oil. When the oil is shimmering, add the chicken and brown both sides in batches, approximately 3 to 4 minutes per side, being careful not to overcrowd the pot. Set chicken aside.

2. Add the garlic and onion and cook approximately 3 to 4 minutes until onions are translucent.

3. Add browned chicken to pot and add patis. Stir so chicken absorbs the patis.

4. Add pineapple juice and chunks, stir until combined.

5. Turn and lock the lid into place, making sure the steam-release valve is in the sealed position. Select Manual and program for 10 minutes on High Pressure. When cooking is complete, quick release pressure manually. Unlock and carefully remove the lid.

6. Add potato, bell pepper, and carrots. Turn and lock the lid into place, making sure the steam-release valve is in the sealed position. Select Manual and program for 0 minutes on High Pressure. When cooking is complete, quick release pressure manually. Unlock and carefully remove the lid.

7. Add evaporated milk and stir. Adjust seasoning with salt and pepper.

TINOLANG MANOK
Chicken Soup in Ginger Broth

Serves 4
Prep Time: 10 minutes
Active Time: 15 minutes
Pressure Cook Time: 10 minutes
Release: Natural + Quick

---

3 tbsp cooking oil

3 cloves garlic, minced

1 small yellow onion, chopped

1 (2-inch piece) ginger,
    thinly sliced

1 lb bone-in chicken pieces
    (thigh, drumsticks, or wings)

3 tbsp patis

4 cups water

2 cups chicken broth

1 green papaya or sayote (chayo-
    te), cut into 1½-inch chunks

3 cups malunggay or spinach

Salt and pepper to taste

Tinolang Manok is a very comforting and healthy dish. It's the perfect meal to eat on a rainy day or to help you get over a bad cold. The chicken is cooked in an aromatic broth with onion, garlic, and ginger. Traditionally, green papaya and malunggay are added to the soup. However, if these ingredients aren't available at your nearest market, you can substitute other veggies such as chayote, potato, or spinach.
-Tisha

1. Preheat the Instant Pot on Sauté setting. When the inner pot is hot, pour in the cooking oil.

2. When the oil is shimmering, add the garlic, onion, and ginger and sweat until aromatic and soft, about 5 minutes.

3. Add chicken, stirring occasionally, about 5 minutes. Add patis and stir until chicken absorbs the patis.

4. Stir in the water and chicken broth.

5. Turn and lock the lid into place, making sure the steam-release valve is in the sealed position. Select Manual and program for 10 minutes on High Pressure. When cooking is complete, allow pressure to release naturally for 10 minutes and then quick release remaining pressure.

6. Unlock and carefully remove the lid. Select Sauté and bring to a boil. Add the green papaya and cook for 4 to 5 minutes until tender.

7. Add malunggay and cook for an additional minute.

8. Adjust seasoning with salt and pepper, serve with rice.

TIP:

If green papaya or chayote is not readily available, you can substitute with potatoes.

AFRITADANG MANOK
Chicken Stew in Tomato Sauce

Serves 3 to 4
Prep Time: 10 minutes
Active Time: 9 minutes
Pressure Cook Time: 10 minutes
Release: Quick

---

3 tbsp cooking oil

4 chicken thighs, quartered

4 cloves garlic, crushed

1 medium onion, chopped

1 (2-inch piece) ginger, minced

1 cup low sodium chicken broth

1 cup tomato sauce

2 hot dogs, sliced

1 celery stalk, halved

3 medium red potatoes, cubed

1 large carrot, cut into
 ½-inch pieces

1 green bell pepper, sliced into
 ½-inch strips

½ cup frozen green peas

3 bay leaves

½ tsp ground black pepper

2 tbsp patis

1 tsp sugar

2 tbsp lemon juice

Salt, pepper, and lemon juice
 to taste

Let's take a moment to thank the Spanish for not just our Hispanic last names but also our variety of meat and tomato sauce stews (afritadang manok being one of the finest). Now, what I really want to know is, why do all these stews have such widely differing names, while sharing 95% of the same steps and ingredients? I mean, how different are afritada, kaldereta, mechado, and menudo? I know there are some nuanced differences, but admit it, you've wondered this too. I find the fact that I'm from a big family of Asians sporting last names like Bautista, Reyes, and de Leon way less confusing. *-Art*

1. Set Instant Pot to Sauté and leave uncovered. Add cooking oil. When the oil is shimmering, add the chicken thighs and brown both sides, about 5 minutes. Set chicken aside.

2. Add garlic, onions, and ginger. Sweat the mixture until aromatic, about 2 minutes.

3. Add chicken thighs, broth, tomato sauce, hot dogs, celery, potatoes, carrot, bell pepper, peas, bay leaves, black pepper, patis, sugar, and lemon juice.

4. Turn and lock the lid into place, making sure the steam-release valve is in the sealed position. Select Manual and program for 10 minutes on High Pressure. When cooking is complete, quick release pressure manually.

5. Unlock and carefully remove the lid. Adjust seasoning with salt, pepper, and lemon juice.

POCHERONG MANOK
Chicken and Saba Banana Stew

Serves 6
Prep Time: 15 minutes
Active Time: 20 minutes
Pressure Cook Time: 12 minutes
Release: Natural

---

5 tbsp cooking oil, divided

3 lbs bone-in chicken pieces
   (thighs, wings, drumsticks)

1 yellow onion, chopped

4 cloves garlic, minced

2 tbsp patis

1 (15 oz) can tomato sauce

1 cup chicken broth

1 tsp ground black pepper

2 chorizo de bilbao, sliced

2 potatoes, cut into
   1½-inch pieces

2 saba bananas, cut into
   1½-inch pieces

1 cup chickpeas

2 cups pechay or bok choy

1 cup green beans

Salt and pepper to taste

I don't recall having this dish until a recent trip to Palm Springs to visit some relatives for dinner. I looked at the spread and noticed there was a dish that looked like chicken afritada at first glance. But then I saw that there was chorizo, chickpeas, and pechay in it. Then, I looked a little closer and saw saba bananas and potatoes. The spiciness from the chorizo and the sweetness of the banana is what left a lasting impression on my taste buds. *-Tisha*

1. Preheat the Instant Pot on Sauté setting. When the inner pot is hot, add 3 tbsp cooking oil. When the oil is shimmering, add the chicken pieces and brown both sides in batches, approximately 3 to 4 minutes per side, being careful not to overcrowd the pot. Set chicken aside.

2. If necessary, add 2 tbsp of cooking oil and add onion and garlic. Sweat until aromatic and soft, about 3 to 4 minutes.

3. Add chicken back to the pot and add patis. Mix until patis evaporates.

4. Add tomato sauce, chicken broth, ground pepper, chorizo de bilbao, potatoes, saba bananas, and chickpeas.

5. Turn and lock the lid into place, making sure the steam-release valve is in the sealed position. Select Manual and program for 12 minutes on High Pressure. When cooking is complete, quick release pressure manually.

6. Unlock and carefully remove the lid. Select Sauté and bring to a boil. Add the pechay and green beans and cook for an additional 3 to 5 minutes until vegetables are tender.

7. Adjust seasoning with salt and pepper, serve with rice.

PINOY CHICKEN CURRY
Filipino-Style Chicken Curry

Serves 4 to 6
Prep Time: 10 minutes
Active Time: 15 minutes
Pressure Cook Time: 8 minutes
Release: Natural

---

2 lbs of boneless, skinless
   chicken thighs

Salt and pepper

1 tbsp cooking oil

8 cloves garlic, minced

1 small onion, chopped

¼ tsp grated ginger

2 tbsp curry powder

3 small potatoes, cut
   into quarters

10 oz baby carrots

1 cup chicken broth

1 tbsp patis

1 (13.5 oz) can full fat coconut
   milk, divided

1 green bell pepper, cut into
   ½-inch slices

I've always enjoyed chicken curry. The bright color makes the dish memorable, but it's the sauce that I really love. The Tamil word "kari" is a generic term used for all sauces. "Curry," popularized by the British, is a derivative of the original "kari." I love the sauce so much that I always finish with a bowl of sauce and rice, no matter how many servings I've had. The yellow curry powder we find in stores is typically made of coriander, turmeric, cumin, fenugreek, and chili pepper. The blend of spices and aromatics, along with the creamy texture of coconut milk, create a fantastic flavor potion for the chicken to stew in. *-Romeo*

1. Season chicken with salt and pepper, and set aside.

2. Preheat the Instant Pot on Sauté setting. When the inner pot is hot, pour in the cooking oil. When the oil is shimmering, add the garlic, onion, and ginger and sweat until aromatic and soft, about 4 minutes.

3. Add curry powder, potatoes, carrots, and chicken, stirring occasionally, about 3 minutes.

4. Stir in the chicken broth, patis, and half of the coconut milk until combined.

5. Turn and lock the lid into place, making sure the steam-release valve is in the sealed position. Select Manual and program for 8 minutes on High Pressure. When cooking is complete, allow pressure to release naturally.

6. Unlock and carefully remove the lid. Select Sauté and bring to a boil. Add bell pepper and cook until tender, about 3 minutes.

7. Turn off Instant Pot. Stir in remaining coconut milk. Adjust seasoning with salt and pepper and serve.

CHAPTER 5

baboy
PORK

SINIGANG NA BABOY
Pork Tamarind Soup

Serves 4 to 6
Prep Time: 8 minutes
Active Time: 5 minutes
Pressure Cook Time: 20 minutes
Release: Natural

---

4 cups water

2 lbs pork butt, cut into
    2-inch cubes

1 onion, quartered

1 firm tomato, quartered

3 tbsp patis

1 packet tamarind sinigang mix

1 Japanese eggplant, cut into
    1-inch wedges

6 bulbs baby bok choy

¼ lb long beans, cut into
    3-inch pieces

Juice of 1 lemon

The Tagalog word "sinigang" means "stewed." Such a generic name is probably why there are so many variations of the dish. I've had it with pork, beef, shrimp, and fish—none ever seeming out of place. Sinigang's distinguishing characteristic is its sourness, although there are different methods to achieve that flavor. Some recipes use fresh tamarind, while others use lemons and tomatoes. When family or friends are hungry, and I need to get food on the table quickly, it's hard to avoid the convenience of a readily available sinigang flavor packet, which has become a staple ingredient in its own right. *-Romeo*

1. Add water, pork, onion, tomato, patis, and sinigang mix into the inner pot.

2. Turn and lock the lid into place, making sure the steam-release valve is in the sealed position. Select Manual and program for 20 minutes on High Pressure. When cooking is complete, allow pressure to release naturally.

3. Remove pork from the inner pot and set aside.

4. In a large bowl and using a sieve, strain the broth and discard solids. Pour strained liquid back into inner pot, and select Sauté.

5. Add eggplant, baby bok choy, and long beans. Cook until eggplant is tender. Approximately 8 to 10 minutes.

6. Remove pork and vegetables from the inner pot, and place into serving bowl.

7. Stir lemon juice into the soup, and pour into serving bowl.

TIP:

Pork spare ribs are a popular meat choice, but I prefer the meat-to-dollar ratio of pork butt. Save time by asking your butcher to cut pork butt into 2-inch cubes.

MENUDONG BABOY
Pork Stew in Tomato Sauce

Serves 4 to 6
Prep Time: 10 minutes
Active Time: 15 minutes
Pressure Cook Time: 18 minutes
Release: Natural

---

2 tbsp cooking oil

4 cloves garlic, minced

1 small onion, diced

2 lbs pork butt or shoulder, cut into 2-inch cubes

¾ cup light sodium soy sauce

2 tbsp patis

1 tbsp ground black pepper

3 bay leaves

¾ cup low sodium chicken broth

1 cup tomato sauce

3 tbsp tomato paste

10 oz baby carrots

3 small potatoes, cut into quarters

Hot dogs and raisins. If I were on a camping trip, the dogs would be on the grill and the raisins in my trail mix. Many Filipinos, though, have no problem pairing these two together. In fact they are essential in Filipino menudo (My lola always included them in hers, and I would pick them out.) Menudo is a hearty, tomato-based meat and potatoes stew. But to be clear, this isn't Mexican menudo, so don't expect it to cure your hangover. Also, don't let my bias cloud your judgment of what should and shouldn't go into menudo. If you love hot dogs and raisins in your stewed pork dishes, toss them in the pot! *-Romeo*

1. Preheat the Instant Pot on Sauté setting. When the inner pot is hot, pour in the cooking oil. When the oil is shimmering, add garlic and onions. Sauté until onions are translucent.

2. Add pork, soy sauce, patis, black pepper, and cook until pork has browned.

3. Add bay leaves and broth. Scrape any bits that have stuck to the bottom of the pot.

4. Add tomato sauce, tomato paste, carrots, and potatoes.

5. Turn and lock the lid into place, making sure the steam-release valve is in the sealed position. Select Manual and program for 18 minutes on High Pressure. Allow pressure to release naturally.

6. Remove bay leaves before serving.

TIP:

Optional Lola-approved ingredients: vienna sausage, pinch of sugar, chickpeas, green peas, and pork liver. These can all be added after step 4, and cooked with the Sauté setting.

ADOBONG BABOY

Pork Adobo

Serves 4 to 6
Prep Time: 10 minutes
Active Time: 10 minutes
Pressure Cook Time: 20 minutes
Release: Natural

---

2 tbsp cooking oil

12 cloves garlic, minced

2 lbs pork butt or shoulder, cut into 2-inch cubes

¾ cup light sodium soy sauce

½ cup apple cider vinegar

1 tbsp patis

4 tsp ground black pepper

4 bay leaves

Lola on my dad's side made it dry, while my other lola made it with plenty of sauce. My uncle used to fry his adobo, and my wife adds boiled eggs to hers. Adobo can be done countless ways, so there is no single "right" way to do it. The type of meat is interchangeable too. The soy sauce to vinegar ratio is negotiable. Anytime I have it, regardless of how anyone makes it, I usually end up liking it. The preserving characteristics of vinegar and salt help adobo keep well, which means baon for work. And if there's any leftover sauce, I don't throw it out; I use it to make adobo fried rice! *-Romeo*

1. Preheat the Instant Pot on Sauté setting. When the inner pot is hot, pour in the cooking oil. When the oil is shimmering, add garlic and sauté until golden.

2. Add pork, soy sauce, vinegar, patis, pepper, and bay leaves.

3. Turn and lock the lid into place, making sure the steam-release valve is in the sealed position. Select Manual and program for 20 minutes on High Pressure. When cooking is complete, allow pressure to release naturally.

4. Remove bay leaves before serving.

PINOY PORK BBQ RIBS
Filipino-Style Pork BBQ Ribs

Serves 6
Prep Time: 15 minutes
Active Time: 10 minutes
Pressure Cook Time: 20 minutes
Release: Natural

2½ lbs pork ribs, cut into smaller sections to ensure they fit in the inner pot for marinating
Salt and ground black pepper

Marinade:
8 cloves garlic, minced
½ cup lemon juice
1 cup soy sauce
1 cup brown sugar
¾ cup ketchup
1 (12 oz) can lemon-lime soda

Spiced Vinegar Dipping Sauce:
1 cup vinegar
2 cloves garlic, minced
2 thai chili peppers, chopped (optional)
¼ tsp ground black pepper

No Filipino party is ever complete without pork barbecue. Typically, thin slices of pork are marinated and skewered on bamboo sticks prior to cooking on a grill. This version uses pork ribs and infuses those same flavors that you're accustomed to when you take a bite of pork barbecue skewers. There's no need to slave over the grill when the Instant Pot does all the work for you. To get a nice caramelization on the ribs, finish them off for a few minutes under a broiler or on the grill. *-Tisha*

1. Remove the membrane from the ribs and generously season both sides with salt and pepper.

2. Combine all the marinade ingredients in the inner pot.

3. Add ribs to marinade, making sure all the ribs are fully coated. Cover and marinate in refrigerator for a minimum of 4 hours or overnight for best results. Turn meat every couple of hours to ensure all the ribs are equally coated.

4. In a small bowl, combine ingredients for spiced vinegar dipping sauce. Cover and set aside.

5. Take the inner pot from the refrigerator when done marinating and place into the Instant Pot. Turn and lock the lid into place, making sure the steam-release valve is in the sealed position. Select Manual and program for 20 minutes on High Pressure. When cooking is complete, allow pressure to release naturally and preheat the broiler. Once pressure has released completely, unlock and carefully remove the lid.

6. Place ribs on a foil-lined sheet pan and spoon leftover marinade sauce from the pot onto the ribs. Broil ribs for 5 to 7 minutes or until brown. Be sure to keep a close watch on the ribs to prevent them from burning.

7. Serve with rice and spiced vinegar dipping sauce.

BICOL EXPRESS
Spicy Pork Stew in Coconut Milk

Serves 4
Prep Time: 5 minutes
Active Time: 7 minutes
Pressure Cook Time: 20 minutes
Release: Natural + Quick

---

3 tbsp cooking oil

10 cloves garlic, minced

1 small onion, diced

1 tbsp grated ginger

12 birds eye chili peppers

2 anaheim peppers

2 lbs pork butt, cut into
  1½-inch cubes

1 tbsp patis

4 tbsp bagoong alamang

¾ cup chicken broth

1½ cups coconut milk

Bicol Express makes me think of a commuter train filled with a bunch of different animals. This recipe has pork butt, shrimp paste, patis, chicken broth, and a partridge in a pear tree. OK, not that last one. Joking aside, the name comes from a train traveling between Manila and Bicol. The Bicol region is known for infusing spicy flavor from chili peppers and using coconut in their dishes. So, as expected, both are present in Bicol Express. *-Romeo*

1. Preheat the Instant Pot on Sauté setting. When the inner pot is hot, pour in the cooking oil. When the oil is shimmering, add garlic, onions, ginger, and peppers. Sauté until garlic is golden.

2. Add pork, patis, and bagoong alamang. Stir until pork is browned. Add chicken broth and scrape any bits that have stuck to the bottom of the pot.

3. Turn and lock the lid into place, making sure the steam-release valve is in the sealed position. Select Manual and program for 20 minutes on High Pressure. When cooking is complete allow pressure to release naturally for 7 minutes and then quick release remaining pressure.

4. Unlock and carefully remove the lid. Select Sauté More, add coconut milk, stir to distribute evenly, and leave uncovered. Reduce sauce down to desired consistency.

DINUGUAN
Pork Blood Stew

Serves 4
Prep Time: 5 minutes
Active Time: 35 minutes
Pressure Cook Time: 20 minutes
Release: Natural

---

3 tbsp olive oil

1½ lbs sliced pork belly, cut into ¾-inch pieces

5 cloves garlic, crushed and peeled

1 medium onion, diced

2 cups water

1 tbsp patis

¾ cup vinegar

3 bay leaves

1 whole jalapeño

2 tsp ground black pepper

1 cup pork blood

Salt, vinegar, and sugar to taste

Call me weird, but as a child, I loved "chocolate meat" more than chocolate ice cream. I wondered how this savory version of chocolate could smell and taste so different from a Hershey bar. I found out one momentous evening, when I watched my mother pour a container of pork blood into a simmering pot and then turn to me and smirk. That was probably the same year I stopped believing in Santa Claus. *-Art*

1. Set Instant Pot to Sauté and add cooking oil to the inner pot. When the oil is shimmering, add pork belly and lightly brown both sides in batches, approximately 5 minutes per side, being careful not to overcrowd the pot. Set pork aside.

2. Add garlic and onions to the inner pot, and scrape any bits that have stuck to the bottom of the pot. Sweat until aromatic, about 2 minutes.

3. Add the pork belly, water, patis, vinegar, bay leaves, jalapeño, and pepper. Turn and lock the lid into place, making sure the steam-release valve is in the sealed position. Select Manual and program for 20 minutes on High Pressure. When cooking is complete, release pressure naturally.

4. Unlock and carefully remove the lid. Select Sauté Less and leave uncovered. Add pork blood and simmer until broth thickens into a gravy.

5. Adjust seasoning with salt, vinegar, and sugar.

TIP:

Turn this recipe into "Crispy Dinuguan" by first pressure cooking large pieces of pork belly on high for 20 minutes then sautéing in oil over high heat until crispy. Slice the crispy pork belly into $^3/_4$-inch pieces and add at the very end.

EMBUTIDO
Filipino-Style Meatloaf

Serves 8
Prep Time: 20 minutes
Active Time: 0 minutes
Pressure Cook Time: 15 minutes
Release: Natural

---

1 lb ground pork

2 eggs

⅓ cup pickle relish

⅓ cup raisins

⅓ cup yellow onion,
   finely chopped

⅓ cup red bell pepper,
   finely chopped

½ cup carrot, finely chopped

½ cup shredded cheddar cheese

1½ tsp salt

½ tsp ground black pepper

1 cup plain bread crumbs

¼ ketchup

3 hot dogs or 8 pieces Vienna
   sausage, cut in half lengthwise

3 hard-boiled eggs, cut in
   quarters lengthwise

1½ cups water

Equipment:

Aluminum foil

Instant Pot trivet

Embutido, a Filipino version of meatloaf, is a dish I enjoy eating with rice and banana ketchup. When you slice into embutido, you are greeted by an abundance of colors from the carrots, bell peppers, raisins, hot dogs and hard-boiled eggs. You can also take these slices and pan fry (along with some eggs) for a quick breakfast, or serve in pandesal for a quick snack. Since it's typically steamed, using an Instant Pot to cook embutido can easily cut your cooking time in half. *-Tisha*

1. In a large bowl, combine the pork and eggs. Then add relish, raisins, onion, bell pepper, carrot, cheese, salt, pepper, bread crumbs, and ketchup. Mix until combined well.

2. Spread ⅓ to ¼ of meat mixture evenly onto a 10-inch by 12-inch piece of foil leaving about a 2-inch space on each side. Place hot dog and hard-boiled eggs in the middle of the flattened meat mixture. Roll the foil so that the meat mixture forms a cylinder, ensuring that the hot dog and egg are in the middle. Fold the edges of foil in to secure the meat mixture in the foil. Note: Make sure you size your embutido to fit into the inner pot. Here are the suggested lengths for the embutido: 8-quart = 8-inch, 6-quart = 7-inch, 3-quart = 6-inch.

3. Continue making embutido until all the meat mixture is used.

4. Add 1½ cups water to the inner pot and place trivet inside. Place embutido rolls on top of the trivet.

5. Turn and lock the lid into place, making sure the steam-release valve is in the sealed position. Select Manual and program for 15 minutes on High Pressure. When cooking is complete, allow pressure to release naturally.

6. Unlock and carefully remove the lid. Using tongs, carefully remove the embutido and place on a plate to cool. Refrigerate for at least 2 hours.

Baboy: It's What's For Dinner
(and Breakfast and Lunch)

From what I understand, a pig is easier and cheaper to raise than other livestock. Unlike a cow, a pig will eat almost anything. And unlike a chicken, it can feed an entire family for several days!

Pork has been an enduring part of Filipino culture since before the Spanish arrived. With pigs being indigenous to the Philippines, our ancestors had time to get things right. They started with their native know-how, sprinkled in some things they learned from visitors and later colonizers, and then forged a rich culinary tradition of Pilipino pork putahe (dishes).

To really hammer home the idea of how important pork is in our cuisine, let's imagine a totally plausible day's worth of meals in the Philippines. For breakfast, we have sinangag (garlic fried rice) with a serving of longganisa, the garlicky, spicy, sticky, slightly sweet, burp-inducing pork link of the islands. For lunch, we'll try some sisig, a sizzling hot platter of chopped pork cheek and ears. Then, for dinner, we're moving on to an entire spit-roasted lechon (it's a special occasion), with the crispiest of skins and a small side of vinegar and sili to cut through the richness of the meat. And finally, for a late-night snack, we're turning those leftovers from dinner into paksiw na lechon, just to make sure we're all porked out.

- Romeo

7. Slice and serve with rice and banana ketchup. If you prefer to eat your embutido hot, feel free to pan fry before serving.

TIPS:

If you don't eat pork, feel free to substitute ground chicken, beef, or turkey.

Freeze leftover embutido in a resealable bag up to 2 months and thaw in the refrigerator when you're ready to eat it.

If you have silicone egg bite molds, you can make single servings by filling each mold halfway with meat mixture, adding sliced hot dog and egg, and then filling the rest of the mold with additional meat mixture.

BINAGOONGANG BABOY
Pork Stewed with Shrimp Paste

Serves 3
Prep Time: 5 minutes
Active Time: 14 minutes
Pressure Cook Time: 25 minutes
Release: Natural + Quick

---

2 cups water, divided

2 tbsp patis

2 tsp ground black
  pepper, divided

1½ lbs pork belly, cut into
  2-inch pieces

3 tbsp cooking oil

5 cloves garlic, crushed

1 medium red onion, diced

½ cup ginisang bagoong

¼ cup vinegar

2 large Chinese eggplant, sliced
  into 1-inch pieces

2 medium tomatoes, chopped

2 bay leaves

1 jalapeño, cut in half lengthwise
  and deseeded

2 tbsp sugar

Salt and sugar to taste

Consider yourself a true Pinay/Pinoy if a pot of crispy pork simmering in fermented shrimp paste excites you. Bonus points if you can properly pronounce "binagoongan." To add depth to this recipe, use a jar of sautéed bagoong, which is brown in color. For our Instant Pot version, the trick to moist pork is to just lightly brown the meat. *-Art*

1. Add 1 cup water, patis, 1 tsp pepper, and pork belly to the inner pot. Turn and lock the lid into place, making sure the steam-release valve is in the sealed position. Select Manual and program for 20 minutes on High Pressure. When cooking is complete, release pressure naturally.

2. Unlock and remove the lid. Remove pork and broth from inner pot, setting broth aside. Clean and dry the inner pot.

3. Select Sauté. When the inner pot is hot, pour in the oil. When the oil is shimmering, add garlic and onion to the inner pot. Sweat the mixture until aromatic, about 2 minutes.

4. Add pork belly and broth that was set aside, remaining cup of water, bagoong, vinegar, eggplant, tomatoes, bay leaves, jalapeño, sugar, and remaining 1 tsp of pepper. Turn and lock the lid into place, making sure the steam-release valve is in the sealed position. Select Manual and program for 5 minutes on High Pressure. When cooking is complete, quick release pressure manually.

5. Unlock and carefully remove the lid. Adjust seasoning with salt and sugar.

TIPS:

For crispier pork belly, after step 2 select Sauté. When the inner pot is hot, pour in the oil. When the oil is shimmering, add pork belly and brown both sides in batches, about 3 to 4 minutes per side. Turn off Instant Pot and set pork aside. Scrape any bits that have stuck to the bottom of the pot. After step 5, stir pork belly into the mixture.

SISIG
Crispy Minced Pork

Serves 4 to 6
Prep Time: 5 minutes
Active Time: 40 minutes
Pressure Cook Time: 20 minutes
Release: Quick

---

1 cup water

2 lb pork belly, cut into
 ½-inch strips

1 lb pig ears

2 bay leaves

1 tsp salt

2 tbsp cooking oil

4 chicken livers, cut into
 ½-inch slices

5 cloves garlic, minced

1 medium red onion, chopped

1 tbsp soy sauce

2 tbsp patis

10 to 14 calamansi, or 2 to 3 lemons, plus more to taste

2 tsp ground black pepper

Salt and pepper to taste

½ stick of butter

Minced hot chilies to taste

1 egg (optional, to crack over top
 of sizzling sisig)

Sisig elevates pork to pulutan (food eaten with alcoholic drinks) perfection. This dish must be boiled, roasted, minced, fried in butter, and served directly from the stove in a sizzling skillet. Serve it to your friends to make sure they understand how truly lucky they are to drink beer and watch pay-per-view at your house! *-Art*

1. Add water, pork belly, pig ears, bay leaves, and salt to inner pot. Select Manual and program for 20 minutes on High Pressure.

2. Meanwhile, add oil to a skillet over medium heat. When the oil is shimmering, sauté liver and garlic, until liver is firm, about 1 to 2 minutes. Mash the liver into small pieces and set aside.

3. When cooking is complete, allow pressure to release naturally for 5 minutes and then quick release remaining pressure. Unlock and carefully remove the lid. Place the cooked belly and ears in a single layer on a foil-lined sheet pan and broil at 450 F until desired crispness, flipping every 3 to 4 minutes.

4. Chop the belly and ears into small cubes.

5. In a large bowl, mix the chopped pork, liver mixture, onions, patis, soy sauce, calamansi juice, and black pepper. Adjust seasoning with salt, pepper, and calamansi juice.

To serve sisig:

Add 1 tbsp of butter to a skillet over medium-high heat for each serving. When the butter shimmers, fry a 1 to 2 cup batch of sisig mixture in pan for 1 to 2 minutes. Serve sisig sizzling in skillet and garnish with chilies and calamansi.

HUMBA

Braised Pork Belly

Serves 6
Prep Time: 15 minutes
Active Time: 15 minutes
Pressure Cook Time: 10 minutes
Release: Natural + Quick

---

3 tbsp cooking oil

2 lbs pork belly, cut into
1½-inch pieces

5 cloves garlic, minced

¼ cup soy sauce

⅓ cup vinegar

1 cup pineapple juice

2 tbsp brown sugar

¼ cup tausi (salted black beans),
drained and rinsed

1 tsp whole black peppercorns

3 bay leaves

½ cup dried banana
blossoms (optional)

Humba is a common dish found in the Visayan Islands and most parts of Mindanao, which are in the southern region of the Philippines. Humba is very similar to pork adobo, as it uses soy sauce and vinegar in the recipe. So if you love adobo, you should try this recipe. It's sweeter than your typical adobo because of the brown sugar and pineapple juice. And what further sets this recipe apart from adobo are the salted black beans and dried banana blossoms. *-Tisha*

1. Preheat the Instant Pot on Sauté setting. When the inner pot is hot, pour in the cooking oil. When the oil is shimmering, add the pork belly and brown all sides for approximately 10 minutes. Add garlic and cook until aromatic.

2. Add soy sauce, vinegar, pineapple juice, brown sugar, tausi, peppercorns, bay leaves, and dried banana blossoms.

3. Turn and lock the lid into place, making sure the steam-release valve is in the sealed position. Select Manual and program for 15 minutes on High Pressure. When cooking is complete, allow pressure to release naturally for 10 minutes and then quick release remaining pressure.

4. Serve with rice.

HAMONADONG BABOY

Pork Belly in Pineapple Syrup

Serves 4 to 6
Prep Time: 5 minutes
Active Time: 22 minutes
Pressure Cook Time: 30 minutes
Release: Quick

---

2 cups pineapple juice

2 lbs pork belly, cut into ½-inch thick strips

2 tbsp soy sauce

2 tbsp sugar

1 tsp cinnamon

1 tsp ground black pepper

2 bitter melon quarters, cored

1 (15 oz) can sliced pineapple

Diabetics, get your insulin ready for this decadent cheat meal. Pork belly stewed in pineapple syrup? Yes, it's really a thing! My weird little trick for balancing the sweetness of this dessert-for-supper cult classic is to add a hint of bitter melon to the syrup. Hear me out... It's the same reasoning behind adding citrus rind or bitters to every grown-up cocktail—bitterness brings the sweetness down to earth. *-Art*

1. Add pineapple juice, pork belly, soy sauce, sugar, cinnamon, black pepper and bitter melon to the inner pot. Turn and lock the lid into place, making sure the steam-release valve is in the sealed position. Select Manual and program for 30 minutes on High Pressure. When cooking is complete, quick release pressure manually.

2. Unlock and carefully remove the lid. Select Sauté and adjust to More mode. Simmer until sauce reduces and sugar bubbles, about 18 to 20 minutes.

3. Turn off Instant Pot. Select Sauté and adjust to Less mode. Remove the bitter melon from the inner pot and discard. Add pineapple slices. Simmer until syrup sticks to the back of a spoon with the thickness of turkey gravy, about 1 to 2 minutes. Be careful not to burn the sugar.

TIP:

Add lemongrass and mint leaves to step 1 for a more Pan-Asian version of the hamonado syrup.

LECHON KAWALI
Crispy Pork Belly

Serves 4 to 6
Prep Time: 10 minutes
Active Time: 20 minutes
Pressure Cook Time: 20 minutes
Release: Natural

---

4 cups water

2 tbsp salt

1 tsp whole black peppercorns

3 bay leaves

8 cloves garlic, crushed

2 lbs pork belly, cut to lay flat in inner pot

Dipping Sauce:

6 tbsp vinegar

2 tbsp soy sauce

1 tbsp white sugar

2 cloves garlic, minced

½ tsp ground black pepper

When it comes to mouth-watering Filipino dishes, lechon kawali ranks at the top of my list. It can be a wonderful appetizer to share or hold its own as a main dish. Typically, the pork is simmered until tender; then deep-fried to a nice crisp. The Instant Pot, when paired with an oven, can achieve the same crispy brown results. Serve with rice and vinegar sawsawan, of course. And if you're having it as an appetizer, nothing pairs better with lechon kawali than an ice cold beer! *-Jorell*

1. Combine water, salt, peppercorns, bay leaves, and garlic in inner pot and add pork belly.

2. Turn and lock the lid into place, making sure the steam-release valve is in the sealed position. Select Manual and program for 20 minutes on High Pressure. When cooking is complete, allow pressure to release naturally.

3. Using tongs, carefully remove pork belly from Instant Pot and lay flat skin side up on a foil-lined sheet pan. Pat both sides with paper towels and allow to air dry for a minimum of 30 minutes or overnight uncovered in the refrigerator.

4. In a small bowl, combine ingredients for dipping sauce and mix until sugar has dissolved.

5. Preheat oven to 450 degrees for 10 minutes. Cook pork belly for 10 to 15 minutes and then flip pork belly over and cook an additional 10 minutes or until brown and crispy.

6. Let cool. Cut into 1-inch pieces and serve with dipping sauce or Sarsa (page 160).

SKINLESS LONGGANISA
Skinless Sweet Pork Sausage

Serves 4
Prep Time: 20 minutes
Active Time: 15 minutes
Pressure Cook Time: 5 minutes
Release: Natural + Quick

---

1 lb ground pork (20 to 30% fat)
2 tsp salt
¼ tsp pepper
1 tsp paprika
8 garlic cloves, finely minced
½ cup brown sugar
¼ cup vinegar
1½ cups water
Cooking oil for frying

Equipment:
Parchment paper
Instant Pot trivet
Aluminum foil

Longganisa, served with garlic fried rice and a fried egg, is one of my favorite Filipino breakfasts. I had no idea how easy it is to make this until I tasted homemade longganisa made by a family friend. Garlic, vinegar, and brown sugar are the key ingredients to this popular breakfast meat. And although you might be missing the bright red color of traditional longganisa, you'll sleep better knowing that this longganisa is free from artificial coloring and preservatives. *-Tisha*

1. In a large bowl, combine ground pork, salt, pepper, paprika, garlic, brown sugar, and vinegar and mix well. Note: it's important to use pork with at least 20% to 30% fat, otherwise the sausage will be dry with leaner meat.

2. To make a longganisa sausage, place 3 tbsp of the meat mixture on 4-inch x 8-inch piece of parchment paper and then roll into a sausage shape. Cut in half so each sausage is 3-inch to 4-inch long. Place the parchment-wrapped sausage in a freezer bag and freeze overnight.

3. To cook, add water to inner pot and place trivet inside. Using foil, make a plate with 1-inch sides that will fit on top of trivet. Remove parchment paper from longganisa and place on foil plate.

4. Turn and lock the lid into place, making sure the steam-release valve is in the sealed position. Select Manual and program for 5 minutes on High Pressure. When cooking is complete, allow pressure to release naturally for 10 minutes and then quick release remaining pressure.

5. Unlock and carefully remove the lid. Take out cooked sausage and carefully discard the foil plate and remove trivet. Empty water from inner pot and dry.

6. Select Sauté setting and add cooking oil to coat the bottom of pot. Add longganisa and cook for approximately 5 minutes or until browned.

IGADONG BABOY
Pork Belly and Liver Stew

Serves 3 to 4
Prep Time: 10 minutes
Active Time: 15 minutes
Pressure Cook Time: 25 minutes
Release: Quick

½ lb pork liver, sliced into
    ¼-inch strips

½ cup soy sauce, divided

½ cup vinegar, divided

3 tbsp cooking oil

5 cloves garlic, minced

1 red onion, diced

1 red bell pepper, sliced into
    ½-inch strips

1 green bell pepper, sliced into
    ½-inch strips

1 lb pork belly, sliced into
    ½-inch strips

1 tbsp patis

4 bay leaves

1 thai chili pepper, whole

½ tsp ground black pepper

1 cup green peas, defrosted

½ tsp oyster sauce

⅓ tsp sinigang powder

Salt and pepper to taste

Liver is a super-food—that is, a super-avoided food—and that's a shame because it is probably one of the most nutritious ingredients in Filipino cooking. Even if your palate is open to pork liver, the hard texture that crumbles in your mouth may ultimately break the deal. The secret to actually making liver enjoyable is to prepare it slightly rare, adding it to the dish last. From there, the fabulous Pinoy flavors will bathe your taste buds and may bring you the rest of the way towards joining "team liver." *-Art*

1. Marinate liver in a medium container with ¼ cup soy sauce and ¼ cup vinegar. Set aside.

2. Preheat the Instant Pot on Sauté setting. When the inner pot is hot, pour in the cooking oil. When the oil is shimmering, add garlic, onions, and bell pepper and sweat until aromatic, about 3 minutes.

3. Add pork belly, patis, bay leaves, thai chili pepper, black pepper. Turn and lock the lid into place, making sure the steam-release valve is in the sealed position. Select Manual and program for 25 minutes on High Pressure. When cooking is complete, quick release pressure manually.

4. Unlock and carefully remove the lid. Add peas, oyster sauce and sinigang powder and stir. Add liver to the top without stirring. Turn and lock the lid into place, making sure the steam-release valve is in the sealed position. Select Manual and program for 0 minutes on Low Pressure. When cooking is complete, quick release pressure manually.

5. Unlock and carefully remove the lid. Stir contents of the pot. Adjust seasoning with salt and pepper.

CHAPTER 6

baka

Beef

left, Nilagang Baka, page 92

NILAGANG BAKA
Beef Soup with Vegetables

Serves 4
Prep Time: 10 minutes
Active Time: 10 minutes
Pressure Cook Time: 20 minutes
Release: Quick

---

2 lbs beef short ribs

1 large onion, halved

1 celery stalk

8 medium red potatoes, halved

2 large carrots, chopped into
   2-inch pieces

2 ears of corn, cut into
   2-inch pieces

6 cups water

2 tbsp patis

1 tbsp ground black pepper

1 cabbage, quartered

Salt to taste

Nilagang Baka is our classic beef and vegetable stew in bone broth. When I was a kid, my bites usually started by dipping my spoon in toyo (and calamansi juice when we had it) and finished with spitting out whole peppercorns. These days, not much has changed, but I do tend to use ground black pepper instead of the whole peppercorns. No more spitting! *-Art*

1. Add short ribs, onion, celery, potatoes, carrots, corn, water, patis, and pepper to the inner pot. Turn and lock the lid into place, making sure the steam-release valve is in the sealed position. Select Manual and program for 20 minutes on High Pressure. When cooking is complete, quick release pressure manually.

2. Unlock and carefully remove the lid. Add cabbage to the inner pot. Select Sauté and simmer uncovered until cabbage is tender, about 7 minutes. Adjust seasoning with salt.

3. Serve with rice and soy sauce and calamansi dipping sauce (in equal parts).

TIP:

Substitute beef short ribs with corned beef—the kind that is marinated with spices and sold in a plastic bag. Pressure cook the corned beef on High in 1 cup of water for 90 minutes before adding the rest of the ingredients.

BULALO
Beef Shank and Marrow Soup

Serves 4
Prep Time: 5 minutes
Active Time: 5 minutes
Pressure Cook Time: 25 minutes
Release: Natural + Quick

---

1 onion, quartered and
layers separated

2½ lbs beef shank

6 beef marrow bones

2 cups water

2 cups low sodium beef broth

4 tbs patis

2 tbsp whole black peppercorns

1 head of broccoli crowns

10 oz package frozen corn kernels

6 bunches baby bok choy

I ordered bone marrow at a high-end restaurant several years ago, and I was extremely disappointed. I also felt cheated because I paid $20 for it! It was nowhere near the glorious experience I had as a kid, when my lola would make nilaga with bone marrow. She would set aside the marrow bones and sprinkle a little salt on them for me. I loved eating every bit of the rich, salty, and custard-like marrow from the bone. Depending on the source, bulalo translates to marrow or knee cap. Fitting, since this simple "cook until tender" dish is made with marrow and beef shank (right above the knee cap). *-Romeo*

1. Place onions, beef shank, marrow bones, water, broth, patis, and peppercorns into the inner pot.

2. Turn and lock the lid into place, making sure the steam-release valve is in the sealed position. Select Manual and program for 25 minutes on High Pressure. When cooking is complete, allow pressure to release naturally for 10 minutes and then quick release remaining pressure.

3. Remove beef and bones from pot and set aside.

4. In a large bowl, strain remaining contents and discard solids. Pour strained liquid in inner pot, and select Sauté.

5. Add broccoli, corn, and bok choy to the inner pot. Cook until broccoli is tender.

MECHADONG BAKA
Tangy Beef Stew in Tomato Sauce

Serves 4 to 6
Prep Time: 5 minutes
Active Time: 45 minutes
Pressure Cook Time: 20 minute
Release: Natural + Quick

---

5 tbsp cooking oil, divided

1½ lbs beef short ribs

5 cloves garlic, crushed

1 medium red onion, diced

½ lbs pork belly, sliced into
   1-inch x ½-inch pieces

3 cups low sodium beef broth

1 cup tomato sauce

¼ cup soy sauce

1 green bell pepper, sliced into
   ½-inch strips

3 to 4 red potatoes, chopped
   into 1-inch cubes

2 medium carrots, cut into
   1-inch pieces

2 bay leaves

2 tsp ground black pepper

1 celery stalk, chopped

1 tbsp patis

Juice of 1 lemon

Salt, lemon juice, and sugar
   to taste

"Mechado" is from the Spanish word "mecha," meaning wick. Traditional mechado calls for strips of pork fat threaded through chunks of beef like candle wicks, making each meaty bite extra indulgent. Our simplified Instant Pot interpretation simply commingles pork and beef in the tomato-based stew. *-Art*

1. Preheat the Instant Pot on Sauté setting. When the inner pot is hot, pour in 3 tbsp cooking oil. When the oil is shimmering, add the short ribs and brown both sides in batches, approximately 7 to 10 minutes per batch, being careful not to overcrowd the pot. Set short ribs aside.

2. Add remaining 2 tbsp oil, garlic, and onions. Scrape any bits that have stuck to the bottom of the pot. Sweat the mixture until aromatic, about 2 minutes.

3. Add short ribs, pork belly, broth, tomato sauce, soy sauce, bell pepper, potatoes, carrots, bay leaves, pepper, celery, patis, and lemon juice, stirring to combine. Turn and lock the lid into place, making sure the steam-release valve is in the sealed position. Select Manual and program for 20 minutes on High Pressure. When cooking is complete, allow pressure to release naturally for 5 minutes and then quick release remaining pressure.

4. Unlock and carefully remove the lid. Adjust seasoning with salt, lemon juice, and sugar.

TIP:

For traditional-style mechado, use beef chuck instead (cut into 2-inch cubes). In each cube, cut a $^3/_4$-inch incision and press a strip of pork fat through using the back of a butter knife to create the "wick."

PICADILLO
Ground Beef Hash with Potatoes, Carrots, and Peas

Serves 8
Prep Time: 15 minutes
Active Time: 15 minutes
Pressure Cook Time: 5 minutes
Release: Natural + Quick

---

3 tbsp cooking oil

2 lbs ground beef

6 cloves garlic, minced

1 medium yellow onion, chopped

3 carrots, diced

2 potatoes, diced

1 (15 oz) can tomato sauce

2 tbsp soy sauce

1 cup raisins

2 cups water

3 tbsp white sugar (optional)

1 cup frozen green peas

Salt and pepper to taste

Picadillo, also known to some as "giniling guisado," is a one-pot dish traditionally enjoyed over rice. Leftovers can be used to make a pandesal sandwich or as a stuffing for empanadas. I remember my college roommate used to bring this home after visiting her parents; and I always looked forward to eating it. I have to admit I didn't even know what this dish was called until a couple of years ago when I wanted to make it for my kids. I love that it includes meat and veggies—perfect for my family. *-Tisha*

1. Preheat the Instant Pot on Sauté setting. When the inner pot is hot, add cooking oil and ground beef. Season with salt and pepper and cook until ground beef is no longer pink.

2. Add garlic, onion, carrots and potatoes and cook for approximately 5 minutes until onions are translucent.

3. Add tomato sauce, soy sauce, raisins, water, and sugar (optional) and mix.

4. Turn and lock the lid into place, making sure the steam-release valve is in the sealed position. Select Manual and program for 5 minutes on High Pressure. When cooking is complete, allow pressure to release naturally for 10 min and then quick release remaining pressure.

5. Unlock and carefully remove the lid. Add green peas and let sit for approximately 5 minutes until peas are completely cooked. Adjust seasoning with salt and pepper and serve over rice.

TIP:

To store for eating later, cool before placing in a freezer container. Cover and freeze for up to 1 to 2 months.

BISTEK
Beef Steak with Onions

Serves 4 to 6
Prep Time: 5 minutes
Active Time: 30+ minutes
Pressure Cook Time: 7 minutes
Release: Natural

¼ cup soy sauce

Juice of 2 lemons, divided

1 cup water, divided

5 cloves garlic, crushed

2 tbsp ground black pepper

3 bay leaves

½ tsp sinigang mix

2 lbs marbled beef, cut into
¼-inch thick strips

5 tbsp cooking oil

1 large onion, sliced into
¼-inch thick rings, divided

1 tsp cornstarch

½ tsp sugar

Lemon juice and sugar to taste

No scoop of rice is safe from the salty, tangy, punch-in-the-face flavor of Bistek. It's one of my go-to plates at turo-turo (cafeteria-style) restaurants, and it has to be topped with a generous pile of greasy onions. Use cuts of beef with marbling to enhance flavor and tenderness. *-Art*

Marinate the beef:

1. In a large bowl, add soy sauce, juice of 1 lemon, $^3/_4$ cup water, garlic, black pepper, bay leaves, sinigang mix, and beef strips. Cover and refrigerate for 30 minutes, or overnight.

2. While beef marinates, preheat the Instant Pot on Sauté setting. When the inner pot is hot, pour in the cooking oil. When the oil is shimmering, add onion and sauté until the edges brown, about 4 to 6 minutes. Set half of the onions aside.

3. Add beef with marinade to the inner pot. Select Manual and program for 7 minutes on High Pressure. While the beef cooks, in a small bowl, combine the cornstarch with the remaining $^1/_4$ cup water.

4. When cooking is complete, release pressure naturally. Unlock and carefully remove the lid. Select Sauté and stir in cornstarch mixture and sugar. Simmer until the sauce sticks to the back of a spoon, about 5 minutes. Adjust seasoning with remaining lemon juice and sugar.

5. Serve on a large platter with remaining sautéed onions.

TIPS:

Ask your butcher to pre-slice the beef into $^1/_4$-inch thick strips to save you some work.

To add more umami flavor, brown the beef in a skillet between steps 2 and 3.

KALDERETANG BAKA
Beef Kaldereta

Serves 4 to 6
Prep Time: 10 minutes
Active Time: 40 minutes
Pressure Cook Time: 20 minutes
Release: Natural

---

5 tbsp cooking oil, divided

2 lbs beef short ribs

5 cloves garlic, crushed

1 medium onion, diced

3 chili peppers, minced

2 cups low sodium beef broth

1 cup tomato sauce

1 green bell pepper, sliced into
  ½-inch strips

3 to 4 red potatoes, chopped
  into 1-inch cubes

2 medium carrots, sliced into
  1-inch pieces

½ cup frozen green peas

½ cup pitted green olives

2 bay leaves

2 tsp ground black pepper

1 celery stalk, sliced into
  ¼-inch pieces

½ cup liver spread

1 tbsp patis

1 tbsp soy sauce

½ tsp sinigang mix

Salt and sugar to taste

Growing up, I experienced kaldereta mainly at parties, although I could never tell if it was kaldereta, afritada, or menudo on my Styrofoam plate. I now know that it's the combination of beef (or goat), spices, and liver that separates kaldereta from the other dishes. This recipe calls for short ribs for a more tender cut of meat and a more flavorful sauce. *-Art*

1. Select Sauté and leave uncovered. When the inner pot is hot, pour in 3 tbsp cooking oil. When the oil is shimmering, add the short ribs and brown both sides in batches, approximately 7 to 10 minutes per batch, being careful not to overcrowd the pot. Set short ribs aside.

2. Add remaining 2 tbsp oil, garlic, onions, and chilies, and scrape any bits that have stuck to the bottom of the pot. Sweat the mixture until aromatic, about 2 minutes.

3. Add short ribs, broth, tomato sauce, bell pepper, potatoes, carrots, peas, olives, bay leaves, black pepper, celery, liver spread, patis, soy sauce, and sinigang mix, stirring until combined. Turn and lock the lid into place, making sure the steam-release valve is in the sealed position. Select Manual and program for 20 minutes on High Pressure. When cooking is complete, allow pressure to release naturally for 5 minutes and then quick release remaining pressure.

4. Unlock and carefully remove the lid. Adjust seasoning with salt and sugar.

KARE-KARE
Beef Stew in Peanut Sauce

Serves 4 to 6
Prep Time: 12 minutes
Active Time: 15 minutes
Pressure Cook Time: 18 minutes
Release: Natural + Quick

---

2 tbsp cooking oil

2 shallots, minced

10 cloves of garlic,
  minced, divided

2½ lbs chuck roast, cut into
  2-inch cubes

3 cups low sodium beef stock

2 tbsp patis

1 tbsp smoked paprika

1 cup creamy peanut butter

2 Japanese eggplant, cut into
  3-inch wedges

6 stalks baby bok choy

½ lb long beans, cut into
  4-inch pieces

3 tbsp bagoong alamang

Watching someone dump a jar of Skippy peanut butter into a pot of meat didn't make sense when I was growing up. That's why I never ate kare-kare as a kid. I finally had kare-kare in adulthood, and it instantly became one of my favorites. The tender, flavorful beef, salty, pungent bagoong alamang, healthy vegetables, and thick creamy peanut-butter-based sauce, come together for a wonderful dish. Word is that it was originally called Kare until the Moro Sultan for whom the dish was first prepared gave it a taste and exclaimed, "It's so nice you gotta say it... twice." -*Romeo*

1. Preheat the Instant Pot on Sauté setting. When the inner pot is hot, pour in the cooking oil. When the oil is shimmering, add shallots and 7 cloves minced garlic. Sauté until garlic is golden.

2. Add beef and lightly brown both sides in batches, about 3 minutes per side, being careful not to overcrowd the pot.

3. Add beef stock, patis, and smoked paprika.

4. Turn and lock the lid into place, making sure the steam-release valve is in the sealed position. Select Manual and program for 18 minutes on High Pressure. Allow pressure to release naturally for 10 minutes and then quick release remaining pressure.

5. Remove beef and place in serving dish.

6. Select Sauté and add vegetables to the inner pot. Cook until eggplant is tender, then transfer vegetables to a serving dish with beef.

7. In the inner pot, add peanut butter to the broth, stirring frequently. Continue cooking until desired consistency is reached.

8. Pour stew into serving dish with beef and vegetables. Serve with bagoong alamang.

NUT-FREE KARE-KARE

Serves 4 to 6
Prep Time: 15 minutes
Active Time: 12 minutes
Pressure Cook Time: 45 minutes
Release: Natural + Quick

---

2 tbsp unrefined coconut oil

2 tbsp garlic, minced

1 large onion, diced

1 tsp salt

½ tsp ground black pepper

3 cups water

2½ lbs oxtail

1 cup unsweetened
   sunflower butter

2 tbsp brown sugar

2 tbsp annatto powder

6 bunches baby bok choy

1 Asian eggplant, cut into
   ½-inch rounds

Bagoong

The prevalence of peanut allergies has increased over time. This is especially sad for those who would like to partake of a steaming bowl of kare-kare. This savory stew of fall-off-the-bone oxtail, chunky veggies, and decadent sauce typically calls for luscious peanut butter, but here, we have substituted peanut butter with sunflower butter for its deep, roasted flavor. Achuete (annatto powder) is added to give the bright orange color, hallmark of kare-kare. Served with a platito of bagoong, your family may never know that it's completely nut-free! *-Jeannie*

1. Preheat the Instant Pot on Sauté setting. When the inner pot is hot, pour in 2 tbsp of coconut oil. When the oil is shimmering, add the garlic and onion and sweat until aromatic and soft, about 2 to 3 minutes.

2. Add salt, pepper, water, and oxtail to the inner pot. Select Meat/Stew setting on High Pressure for 45 minutes.

Prepare the sauce:

3. While the oxtail is cooking, place a small saucepan on the stove over medium heat. Add sunflower butter. When sunflower butter has melted, stir in brown sugar.

4. Gently sprinkle annatto powder into sunflower butter mixture and stir, ensuring that the powder thoroughly dissolves (no lumps). Set aside.

5. When cooking time on the Instant Pot is complete, let the pressure release naturally for 10 minutes then quick release the remaining pressure manually. Unlock and carefully remove the lid and gently stir sunflower butter sauce into the broth. Avoid disturbing the oxtail too much.

6. Add the vegetables. Select Sauté setting and cover with a glass lid. Cook vegetables to your desired softness.

7. Serve as desired with a side of bagoong.

recipe continues >

NUT FREE
KARE-KARE

continued >

TIPS:

Our recipe calls for unrefined coconut oil to add fragrance, but you may substitute with a cooking oil of your choice.

Annatto powder is preferable to annatto seeds. If annatto powder isn't available near you, you may substitute it with annatto seeds. Procedure: Soak $\frac{1}{4}$ cup of annatto seeds in $\frac{1}{2}$ cup of warm oxtail broth for 5 minutes. Massage the seeds with a fork or your fingers to extract as much color as possible. (Wear food-grade gloves to avoid staining your hands.) Strain the mixture. Discard the seeds and add the annatto mixture to the kare-kare sauce in step 4 after melting the sunflower butter.

We have included brown sugar in this recipe for mild sweetness and deeper color. White sugar may be substituted. If you use a pre-sweetened sunflower butter, then omit sugar.

If you prefer your vegetables al dente, you may blanch them in a separate pot and serve on the side of your kare-kare.

MEATBALL SHANGHAI
Lumpia-Inspired Meatballs

16 meatballs
Prep Time: 15 minutes
Active Time: 0 minutes
Pressure Cook Time: 4 minutes
Release: Natural

½ lb ground beef
½ lb ground pork
¼ cup grated onion
¼ cup grated carrot
1 thumb ginger, grated
⅛ cup soy sauce
1 tsp patis
¾ tsp ground black pepper
¾ tsp garlic powder
½ cup cilantro, chopped
½ cup water chestnuts, diced
1 egg
½ cup panko breadcrumbs
1 cup water

Equipment:
Instant Pot trivet

Ever crave lumpia but were too lazy to deep fry them? Peeled the wrapper off the lumpiang shanghai just to eat the meat? This dish is pretty much "naked lumpiang shanghai"—just the meat, sans wrapper. Our recipe calls for ground pork and beef, but you can substitute ground chicken or turkey. Try pairing these meatballs with banana ketchup or sweet chili sauce or eating them in a lettuce wrap. *-Jeannie*

1. In a large mixing bowl, put all ingredients except breadcrumbs and mix until well integrated.

2. Fold the breadcrumbs into the meat mixture until completely combined.

3. Roll the meat into 1½-inch balls. Set aside.

4. Add water to the inner pot and place trivet inside. Place meatballs on trivet, double-stacking the balls if needed (they will not stick upon cooking).

5. Turn and lock the Instant Pot lid into place, making sure the steam-release valve is in the sealed position. Select Manual and program for 4 minutes on High Pressure. When cooking is complete, turn off Instant Pot and release pressure naturally.

6. Unlock, carefully remove the lid and the meatballs.

7. Serve with Banana Ketchup (page 156) or sweet chili sauce.

For Lettuce Wraps:

8. Separate leaves from a small head of butter lettuce, then rinse and dry well.

9. Fill each leaf with plain coleslaw mix (available in salad section of your grocery) or bean sprouts.

10. Place 1 to 2 meatballs in each lettuce cup.

11. Top with sweet chili sauce or sauce of your choice.

TAPA

Citrus-Soy Cured Beef

Serves 4 to 6

Prep Time: 12 minutes, plus
marinate overnight

Active Time: 10 minutes

Pressure Cook Time: 8 minutes

Release: Quick

½ cup low sodium soy sauce

¼ cup lemon juice

¼ cup lime juice

5 tbsp cooking oil, divided

1 tsp ground black pepper

1 head of garlic, chopped

2 lbs chuck roast, cut into
¼-inch slices

Throughout my life, I've heard this dish called tapa, pindang, even bistek, so I was never sure of its actual name. But growing up, I primarily knew it as pindang and ate it regularly for breakfast with rice. Tapa is basically sliced beef, marinated in soy sauce and citrus, but my childhood version was made with onions cooked through, and barely any sauce. This recipe has neither onions, nor sauce, but it does pack plenty of flavor. Check the tips section for alternate ingredients. *-Romeo*

1. In a large mixing bowl, mix soy sauce, lemon juice, lime juice, 2 tbsp cooking oil, black pepper, brown sugar, and garlic.

2. Combine beef and marinade in a large resealable bag. Place in refrigerator and marinate overnight.

3. Place beef and marinade into the inner pot.

4. Turn and lock the lid into place, making sure the steam-release valve is in the sealed position. Select Manual and program for 8 minutes on High Pressure. When cooking is complete, quick release pressure manually.

5. Set aside contents, and wipe inner pot dry.

6. Select Sauté, add remaining 3 tbsp cooking oil. When inner pot is hot and oil is shimmering, add beef and fry until a slight crust forms.

TIPS:

Save time by asking your butcher to cut the beef into $^1/_4$-inch thick slices.

Add $^1/_2$ tsp of brown sugar to the marinade, if you'd like a little sweetness to your tapa.

Add more black pepper ($^1/_2$ tbsp), as well as 8 chopped sili labuyo (bird's eye chili) and 1 tbsp Tabasco sauce to the marinade for a bit of heat.

CHAPTER 7

Lamandagat
Seafood

SINIGANG NA SALMON
Salmon Tamarind Soup

Serves 3 to 4
Prep Time: 15 minutes
Active Time: 15 minutes
Pressure Cook Time: 5 minutes
Release: Quick

---

1 salmon head

1½ lbs salmon belly, cut into 1-inch strips

3 tbsp cooking oil

1 large onion, quartered

3 cloves of garlic, crushed

1 (2-inch piece) ginger, cut into ⅛-inch slices

2 medium tomatoes, quartered

4 (14.5 oz) cans low sodium chicken broth

2 cups water

3 small taro root, cut into 1-inch thick slices

1 jalapeño, cut in half lengthwise and deseeded

1 tbsp patis

¼ tsp ground black pepper

1 (1.4 oz) packet sinigang mix

¼ lb green beans

¼ lb okra

5 bunches baby bok choy

Salt and sinigang mix to taste

I fell in love with salmon belly sinigang because of its melt-in-your-mouth softness—what an upgrade from pork! When salmon belly wasn't in our budget, salmon head would do. I learned that enjoying salmon head is about going for it. Pull it apart and suck out all of its secrets until there's nothing left but a loose pile of fish bones. *-Art*

1. Pat the salmon head and belly dry with a paper towel. Season with salt and pepper and set aside.

2. Preheat the Instant Pot on Sauté setting. When the inner pot is hot, pour in the cooking oil. When the oil is shimmering, add onion, garlic, ginger, and sweat until aromatic, about 2 to 3 minutes.

3. Add tomatoes and sauté until tender, about 5 minutes.

4. Add salmon head, broth, water, taro, jalapeño, patis, pepper, ½ of the sinigang mix, green beans, and okra. Select Manual and program for 5 minutes on High Pressure. When cooking is complete, quick release pressure manually.

5. Unlock and carefully remove the lid. Select Sauté and adjust to Less mode. Add salmon belly and bok choy. Simmer uncovered until bok choy is tender, about 7 minutes. Adjust seasoning with salt and sinigang mix.

SINIGANG NA HIPON
Shrimp Tamarind Soup

Serves 4 to 6
Prep Time: 15 minutes
Active Time: 10 minutes
Pressure Cook Time: 0 minutes
Release: Quick

---

2 tbsp cooking oil

1 small yellow onion, chopped

2 tomatoes, quartered

6 cups water

1 (6-inch piece) daikon, sliced

¼ lb green beans, cut into
   2-inch pieces

1 (1.4 oz) packet sinigang mix

2 Japanese eggplants, cut into
   2-inch wedges

2 banana peppers (optional)

1 lb shrimp with shell on

3 cups spinach

Patis to taste

Sinigang is one of the most popular and versatile dishes in Filipino cuisine. Its sour flavor is derived from sampalok (tamarind), and can be prepared with a variety of proteins and vegetables. Pork sinigang is probably the most common version, but sinigang na hipon (shrimp) is a family favorite. As with most seafood prepared in the Instant Pot, this cooks rather quickly. Although pre-packaged sinigang mix makes it quite convenient, you can also use tamarind paste for the soup base. We prefer it more on the sour side, so play around with it and find your desired sourness! *-Jorell*

1. Preheat the Instant Pot on Sauté setting. When the inner pot is hot, pour in the cooking oil. When the oil is shimmering, add the onion and tomato cooking until soft, about 3 to 4 minutes. Add water, daikon, green beans, and sinigang mix and stir.

2. Turn and lock the lid into place, making sure the steam-release valve is in the sealed position. Select Manual and program for 0 minutes on High Pressure. When cooking is complete, quick release pressure manually.

3. Unlock and carefully remove the lid. Select Sauté and bring to a boil. Add the eggplant and banana peppers and cook for 3 minutes.

4. Add the shrimp and cook for about 3 minutes, or until they turn pink. Turn off Instant Pot and stir in the spinach.

5. Adjust seasoning with patis and serve with rice.

SINIGANG NA ALIMANGO
Crab Tamarind Soup

Serves 3 to 4
Prep Time: 10 minutes
Active Time: 20 minutes
Pressure Cook Time: 7 minutes
Release: Quick

---

3 tbsp olive oil

3 cloves of garlic, crushed

1 large red onion, quartered

1 (2-inch piece) ginger, sliced

2 medium tomatoes, quartered

2 cups water, divided

3 small taro root, cut into
    1-inch slices

1 dungeness crab, cleaned

4 (14.5 oz) cans low sodium
    chicken broth

1 bunch broccoli, cut into florets

1 Chinese eggplant, cut into
    1-inch slices

1 jalapeño, cut in half lengthwise
    and deseeded

1 (1.4 oz) packet of sinigang
    mix, divided

1 tbsp patis

¼ tsp ground black pepper

Salt and sinigang mix
    to taste

1 bunch mustard leaves, cut into
    2-inch strips

My mom told me that children who eat the crab's gills become smarter than children who don't. I eagerly gobbled up every last crab gill put in front of me for years until I became smart enough to realize that my mom was just pulling my leg. This recipe is a sinigang variation that celebrates that old memory, gills and all. *-Art*

1. Preheat the Instant Pot on Sauté setting. When the inner pot is hot, pour in the cooking oil. When the oil is shimmering, add the garlic, onion, and ginger and sweat until aromatic, about 2 to 3 minutes.

2. Add tomatoes and sauté until tender, about 5 minutes.

3. Add 1 cup of water to the inner pot and place trivet inside. Add taro and crab. Turn and lock the lid into place. Select Manual and program for 3 minutes on High Pressure. When cooking is complete, quick release pressure manually.

4. Unlock and carefully remove the lid. Remove trivet and crab and let cool. Detach the legs and claws from the crab body and set them aside. Place the crab body back into the inner pot.

5. Add 1 cup of water, broth, eggplant, jalapeño, half of the packet of sinigang mix, patis, pepper. Turn and lock the lid into place, making sure the steam-release valve is in the sealed position. Select Manual and program for 4 minutes on High Pressure. When cooking is complete, quick release pressure manually.

6. Unlock and carefully remove the lid. Select Sauté and adjust to Less mode. Add broccoli and mustard leaves and simmer uncovered until tender, about 5 to 7 minutes. Add crab claws and legs to broth. Adjust seasoning with salt and sinigang mix.

GINATAANG HIPON
Whole Shrimp in Coconut Cream

Serves 4 to 6
Prep Time: 10 minutes
Active Time: 5 minutes
Pressure Cook Time: 0 minutes
Release: Quick

---

2 tbsp cooking oil

3 tbsp garlic, minced

½ cup red onion, sliced

1 (2-inch piece) ginger, grated

1 (19 oz) can coconut cream

2 tbsp patis

2 chili peppers (optional)

1 lb whole shrimp or prawns

½ tsp ground black pepper

My mom taught me to be frugal and save money, so I sometimes feel guilty about ordering shrimp when eating out. I feel completely guilt-free, however, about making this ginataang hipon at home; it's loaded with flavor and texture. Traditionally, Filipinos like shrimp with heads on, as the heads contain the rich, tasty organs of the shellfish. You can replace fresh shrimp with frozen shrimp if you prefer. *-Jeannie*

1. Preheat the Instant Pot on Sauté setting. When the inner pot is hot, pour in the cooking oil. When the oil is shimmering, add the garlic, onion, and ginger, and sweat until aromatic and soft. Turn off Instant Pot.

2. Add remaining ingredients into the inner pot. Turn and lock the lid into place, making sure the steam-release valve is in the sealed position. Select Manual and program for 0 minutes on High Pressure. When cooking is complete, quick release pressure manually.

TIPS:

Serve with garlic fried rice or coconut rice.

For a low-carb option, try serving with Japanese shirataki noodles, which are made of a Japanese root vegetable called konnyaku. In a skillet, brown 4 tbsp of butter over medium heat. Sauté 2 tbsp of minced garlic in the butter. Then, warm 2 packages of noodles in the garlic butter. Platter noodles and place one serving of shrimp on top.

PAKSIW NA ISDA
Whole Fish Simmered in Vinegar

Serves 3 to 4
Prep Time: 40 minutes
Active Time: 0 minutes
Pressure Cook Time: 8 minutes
Release: Quick

---

1 large bitter melon, cut in half lengthwise and deseeded

3¼ cups water, divided

1 tbsp salt

1½ lb whole fish (bangus, tilapia, pompano, or trout)

½ cup + 2 tbsp vinegar

1½ tbsp patis

¾ tsp ground black pepper

½ tsp sinigang mix

5 cloves garlic, crushed

1 small red onion, sliced

1 (4-inch piece) ginger, sliced

1 stalk lemongrass, with leaves, root, and outer skin removed

1 jalapeño, cut in half lengthwise and deseeded

1 medium Japanese eggplant, cut into 1-inch pieces

2 tbsp butter

Water, vinegar, and salt to taste

My lola, my titas, and my mom love paksiw na isda. There always seems to be a pot of it in their kitchens. When I was younger, I'd meekly pass on it and go for something easier like Spam or salted eggs. I couldn't get over how un-sugarcoated the ingredients were: bitter melon, bony bangus, eggplant, slices of ginger, hot pepper, and vinegar. As I boldly stride out of my youth, I'm feeling this dish, sharp bones and all. I think it takes the self-acceptance that comes with age to love a dish so unapologetic and authentically Filipino. *-Art*

Prepare the bitter melon:

1. Slice bitter melon into ¼-inch pieces. In a medium container, add 2 cups water, salt, and bitter melon. Stir until salt dissolves. Soak for 30 minutes. When soaking is done, discard salt water and set bitter melon aside.

Marinate the fish:

2. While bitter melon soaks, add fish, 1¼ cup water, vinegar, patis, black pepper, sinigang mix, garlic, onion, ginger, and lemongrass to inner pot. Marinate for 30 minutes.

3. Add bitter melon, jalapeño, eggplant, and butter to inner pot. Turn and lock the lid into place, making sure the steam-release valve is in the sealed position. Select Manual and program for 8 minutes on Low Pressure. When cooking is complete, quick release pressure manually.

4. Unlock and carefully remove the lid. Adjust seasoning with water, vinegar, or salt.

5. Serve with rice.

SARDINAS NA BANGUS
Spanish Sardine-Style Milkfish

Serves 6
Prep Time: 10 minutes
Active Time: 0 minutes
Pressure Cook Time: 25 minutes
Release: Quick

---

2 lbs bangus (milk fish), scaled and cut into 1½-inch pieces
1 medium carrot, sliced
½ cup olives
2 thai chili peppers, sliced
3 bay leaves
½ cup olive oil
⅓ cup water
½ tsp peppercorn
1 tsp salt

I grew up in a household where we consumed fish on a regular basis. We ate it fried, steamed, in sinigang (tamarind soup), for breakfast with rice and eggs, or straight out of the can. My dad has always been a big fan of canned sardines so he always keeps a stash of it stocked in their pantry. Whenever he craves sardinas na bangus, my mom makes this recipe for him so he can enjoy eating it for the rest of the week. *-Tisha*

1. Put all ingredients into the inner pot and give it a quick stir. Make sure the bangus is submerged in the liquid. If needed, add a little additional water and cooking oil.

2. Turn and lock the lid into place, making sure the steam-release valve is in the sealed position. Select Manual and program for 25 minutes on High Pressure. When cooking is complete, quick release pressure manually.

3. Serve with rice.

TALABA NA MAY KINILAW

Ceviche-Topped Oysters

Serves 2 to 3
Prep Time: 10 minutes
Active Time: 5 minutes
Pressure Cook Time: 3 minutes
Release: Quick

---

8 oysters

1 cup water

½ cup red onion, minced

6 chive stems, minced

2 (2-inch pieces) ginger, minced

¼ medium green mango, peeled and minced (optional)

Juice of 10 Calamansi / 5 limes

5 tsp vinegar

½ thai chili pepper, seeded and minced

6 tbsp coconut cream

2 pinches salt

2 pinches ground black pepper

2 stems cilantro

Calamansi juice and Tabasco sauce, as needed

Equipment:
Instant Pot trivet

If you've ever struggled to cook oysters just right, you will be amazed by the speed and consistency of steaming them in the Instant Pot. The topping is inspired by kinilaw, aka Filipino ceviche. *-Art*

1. Add water to the inner pot and place trivet inside. Place oysters on trivet. Select Manual and program for 3 minutes on High Pressure. When cooking is complete, quick release pressure manually.

2. Unlock and carefully remove the lid. Remove oysters and set aside to cool.

3. Open each oyster and cut the connecting vein, leaving each oyster on the half shell.

Prepare the topping:

4. In a medium bowl, add remaining ingredients and mix well.

5. Use 1 tbsp of topping per oyster. Serve with calamansi juice and Tabasco sauce.

TIP:

The oysters will overcook quickly, so don't forget to drop what you're doing and quick release the pressure!

Food of Nine Seas

The Philippines is an archipelago made up of over 7600 islands and surrounded by nine different seas. Located in the Indo-Pacific geographic region, it's renowned throughout the world for its unrivaled marine species biodiversity. So it's no wonder Filipinos have, since ancient times, relied on seafood as a major source of protein, with over half the population eating some form of fish every day. In fact, due to the tropical climate, early Filipinos even developed methods of dehydrating, salting, and smoking to preserve and fight spoilage in seafood.

My mother and her six siblings grew up in a seaside village in northern Cebu. Coming from humble beginnings in the post-World War II era, she remembers not having much protein to eat because money was tight. Her mom, my lola, would divide cooked rice and fish (or other ulam) into equal portions, and the kids would line up to get their share of the meal. Sometimes, Lola would then set aside any remaining food for an unexpected guest who might drop by.

For my mom and her siblings, these memories have made seafood a form of comfort food. To this day, their faces light up when they receive pasalubong of fish from a balikbayan (a returning Filipino). They especially love danggit (dried fish) and dried pusit (squid)—delicacies of their region, which, when dipped in sukang maanghang, adds pungent, salty flavor to plain rice or lugaw.

So, there are a lot of reasons why I love seafood, and I didn't even mention how good it is for you. It provides a better omega-3 to omega-6 fatty acid ratio than most meats, which is less inflammatory to the body and assists with cardiovascular function and brain development. But health benefits aside, seafood is just plain sarap.

-Jeannie

CHAPTER 8

Gulay
Veggies

MONGGO GUISADO
Mung Bean Stew

Serves 4
Prep Time: 10 minutes
Active Time: 5 minutes
Pressure Cook Time: 12 minutes
Release: Natural

¾ cup chicharon

2 tbsp coconut oil

1 tbsp garlic, minced

½ cup chopped onion

½ cup dried shrimp

½ cup cherry tomatoes, halved

1 cup mung beans, rinsed

3 cups water

3 cups baby spinach

Patis, salt, and black pepper
   to taste

Monggo guisado is a comforting stew, loaded with textures and flavors to please the palate: pasty beans, melt-in-your-mouth spinach, salty shrimp and patis. We've added tomatoes in this recipe for pleasing pops of red color and mild acid. This dish can be served à la carte or over rice. It's perfect for dinner at home while watching Netflix in your favorite pajamas! *-Jeannie*

1. In a resealable plastic or silicone bag, break chicharon into $1/2$ to 1-inch pieces with a rolling pin and set aside.

2. Preheat the Instant Pot on Sauté setting. When the inner pot is hot, pour in the coconut oil. When the oil is shimmering, add the garlic and onion and sweat until aromatic and soft. Turn off Instant Pot.

3. Add the crushed chicharon, dried shrimp, tomatoes, beans, and water.

4. Turn and lock the lid into place, making sure the steam-release valve is in the sealed position. Select Bean/Chili mode and program for 12 minutes on High Pressure. When cooking is complete, release pressure naturally.

5. Unlock lid and add spinach, which will wilt immediately in the hot stew.

6. Adjust seasoning with patis, salt, and black pepper.

TIPS:

A half pound of fresh shrimp may be substituted for dried shrimp. Sauté them at step 2 with the garlic and onions until just cooked and set the shrimp aside. Add them back into the pot after wilting the spinach at step 5.

For vegetarian options, omit shrimp and chicharon and substitute liquid aminos for patis. Deep-fried tofu or smoked tofu may be added.

GINISANG UPO
Sautéed Bottle Gourd

Serves 4
Prep Time: 20 minutes
Active Time: 8 minutes
Pressure Cook Time: 4 minutes
Release: Quick

---

2 large upo squashes (7 to 10 inches long)

1 tbsp olive oil

6 cloves garlic, minced

2 small onions, chopped

1 lb of ground pork

Light pinch of salt

Light pinch of ground black pepper

2 tbsp patis

3 medium tomatoes, diced

Salt and pepper to taste

Sautéed upo is one of the first dishes my mom ever cooked for my dad when they started dating. He loved it, and from then on, would ask her to make it every time he visited her. To this day, she swears it's what has kept them together. So of course, I now cook it for my wife regularly, just for good measure.

Cleaning and deseeding upo takes some time, but once you're done, the Instant Pot does its thing, infusing salty, porky, garlicky goodness into a nutritious veggie dish that even the kiddies will love. *-Jaymar*

1. Begin preparing the upo by cutting off the ends and slicing the gourds in half long ways.

2. Remove the seeds and spongy white filling. Peel and chop into 1-inch pieces.

3. Preheat the Instant Pot on Sauté setting. When the inner pot is hot, pour in the olive oil. When the oil is shimmering, add the garlic and onions, and sweat until aromatic and soft, about 4 minutes.

4. Add the ground pork. Lightly season with salt and pepper, and sauté until lightly brown. Stir in the patis.

5. Add the upo and tomato. Give the vegetables and meat a quick stir to get them evenly distributed, then turn off the Instant Pot.

6. Turn and lock the lid into place, making sure the steam-release valve is in the sealed position. Select Manual and program for 4 minutes on High Pressure. When cooking is complete, quick release pressure manually.

7. When steam is fully released, unlock and carefully remove the lid. Select Keep Warm and stir to distribute liquids evenly throughout the pot.

8. Adjust seasoning with salt and pepper and serve.

GINISANG AMPALAYA AT HIPON

Sautéed Bitter Melon and Shrimp

Serves 3 to 4
Prep Time: 35 minutes
Active Time: 15 minutes
Pressure Cook Time: 0 minutes
Release: Quick

---

2 bitter melons, cut in half
  lengthwise and deseeded

2 cups water

1 tbsp salt

3 tbsp cooking oil

4 cloves garlic, crushed

1 red onion, chopped

¼ cup low sodium chicken broth

3 cups cherry tomatoes

1 tbsp patis

1 tsp ground black pepper

1 tbsp lemon juice

20 frozen raw prawns

2 eggs, beaten

Salt and pepper to taste

Your reaction to bitter melon can predict how Filipino you are. An aversion may indicate that your grandparents were born in the Philippines and you and your parents were not. A taste for bitter melon may reveal that you understand basic Tagalog and have eaten a few balut in your day. Finally, a LOVE of bitter melon strongly correlates to your skill of maneuvering a motorized tricycle through Manila traffic. *-Art*

Prepare the bitter melon:

1. Slice bitter melon into $\frac{1}{4}$-inch pieces. In a medium container, add 2 cups water, salt, and bitter melon. Stir until salt dissolves. Soak for 30 minutes. When soaking is done, discard salt water and set bitter melon aside.

2. Set Instant Pot to Sauté and leave uncovered. When the inner pot is hot, pour in the cooking oil. When the oil is shimmering, add garlic and onions and sweat until aromatic and soft, about 2 minutes.

3. Add broth, tomatoes, patis, pepper, and lemon juice. Simmer until tomatoes soften, about 5 minutes. Break tomatoes open with a large spoon.

4. Add bitter melon and prawns. Turn and lock the lid into place, making sure the steam-release valve is in the sealed position. Select Manual and program for 0 minutes on Low Pressure. When cooking is complete, quick release pressure immediately. Unlock and carefully remove the lid. Remove prawns and set aside.

5. Set Instant Pot to Sauté and leave uncovered. Simmer until broth reduces below the vegetables, stirring occasionally, about 3 to 5 minutes.

6. Add beaten eggs. Stir until the eggs fully curdle, about 1 to 2 minutes. Adjust seasoning with salt and pepper. Add cooked prawns and serve.

ADOBONG CAULIFLOWER

Cauliflower Adobo

Serves 4
Prep Time: 6 minutes
Active Time: 2 minutes
Pressure Cook Time: 2 minutes
Release: Quick

¾ cup white vinegar

½ cup dark soy sauce

1 tbsp brown sugar

1 large cauliflower, cut into
  6 wedges

3 tbsp cooking oil

3 tbsp garlic, minced

½ large onion, sliced

2 bay leaves

½ tsp ground black pepper

You might consider vegetarian adobo to be possibly heresy, or worse, hipster. But using cauliflower in lieu of meat allows folks with dietary preferences, like vegetarian or vegan, to enjoy adobo as their ulam with a side of rice. We set the cook time to give the cauliflower al dente consistency. *-Art*

1. In a small bowl, mix vinegar, soy sauce, and brown sugar using a whisk until well combined and set aside.

2. In a large bowl, place cauliflower wedges and pour adobo sauce over them. Toss until fully dressed.

3. Preheat the Instant Pot on Sauté setting. When the inner pot is hot, pour in the cooking oil. When the oil is shimmering, add the garlic, onion, and bay leaves and sweat until aromatic and soft, about 4 minutes.

4. Add the cauliflower wedges, sauce, and black pepper into the inner pot. Turn and lock the lid into place, making sure the steam-release valve is in the sealed position. Select Manual and program for 2 minutes on Low Pressure. When cooking is complete, quick release pressure manually.

5. Unlock and carefully remove the lid. Carefully transfer the wedges to a serving plate. Baste broth over cauliflower.

TIPS:

$1/2$ cup of firm tofu (cubed) can be added to this recipe for more protein.

$1/2$ cup of sliced mushrooms (e.g., portabella or shiitake) can be added to enhance flavor.

For keto followers, replace the brown sugar with a stevia and erythritol sweetener, such as Truvia.

GINATAANG LANGKA
Green Jackfruit in Coconut Cream

Serves 4

Prep Time: 10 minutes

Active Time: 5 minutes

Pressure Cook Time: 6 minutes

Release: Quick

---

2 (20 oz) cans green jackfruit (in water)

2 tbsp cooking oil

2 tbsp garlic, minced

1 small onion, diced

1 (2-inch piece) ginger, minced

½ lb pork belly, cut into ½-inch pieces

1 (14 oz) can coconut cream

1½ tbsp patis

¼ tsp salt

¼ tsp ground black pepper

2 tbsp bagoong (optional)

2 chili peppers (optional)

Langka, or jackfruit, is a tropical fruit commonly used in South and Southeast Asian cuisine. It's the largest fruit in the world and can grow to 100 pounds or more. Jackfruit provides fiber, protein, and numerous vitamins and antioxidants. The flesh of the ripe fruit is fragrant and tangy, while the unripe fruit is green and mildly acidic. The green jackfruit has grown in popularity among vegetarians as its texture mimics that of pulled pork. This ginataang langka can be cooked with or without pork, patis, or bagoong. If included, the bagoong will give the dish a light pink color. *-Jeannie*

Prepare the jackfruit:

1. Remove from can and slice into 1-inch pieces. Wrap a small handful of jackfruit in a paper towel or cheesecloth and squeeze out as much brine as possible. Repeat for the remaining jackfruit. Place jackfruit in a strainer and set aside.

2. Preheat the Instant Pot on Sauté setting. When the inner pot is hot, pour in the cooking oil. When the oil is shimmering, add the garlic, onion, and ginger and sweat until aromatic and soft.

3. Add pork to pot and cook until well done. Turn off Instant Pot.

4. Add remaining ingredients to the inner pot. Stir to combine.

5. Turn and lock the lid into place, making sure the steam-release valve is in the sealed position. Select Manual and program for 6 minutes on High Pressure. When cooking is complete, quick release pressure manually.

TIP:

For a vegetarian option, omit pork and substitute liquid aminos for patis and bagoong.

GINATAANG PUSO NG SAGING
Banana Blossom in Coconut Cream

Serves 4
Prep Time: 10 minutes
Active Time: 5 minutes
Pressure Cook Time: 3 minutes
Release: Quick

---

2 (20 oz) cans banana blossom
   (in brine)

2 tbsp cooking oil

1 tbsp garlic, minced

1 small onion, diced

1 (1-inch piece) ginger, minced

½ cup coconut cream

1 tbsp patis

½ tbsp rice wine vinegar

¼ cup chicken broth

¼ tsp salt

1 pasilla pepper, seeded
   and diced

½ lb frozen shrimp, shells on

Calamansi juice and patis
   to taste

Ground black pepper to taste

Puso ng saging translates to "heart of the banana." It really is the giant flower of a banana tree, also called a banana blossom. When cooked as a savory dish, the banana blossom texture is similar to langka (jackfruit). Imagine a chewy artichoke. Like jackfruit, banana blossom makes a great meat alternative and absorbs flavors from the accompanying sauce. *-Jeannie*

1. Remove the blossom from the can and slice into 1-inch pieces. Wrap a small handful of blossom in a paper towel or cheesecloth and squeeze out as much brine as possible. Repeat for remaining blossom. Place blossom in a strainer and set aside.

2. Preheat the Instant Pot on Sauté setting. When the inner pot is hot, pour in the cooking oil. When the oil is shimmering, add the garlic, onion, and ginger and sweat until aromatic and soft. Turn off Instant Pot.

3. Add the banana blossom, coconut cream, patis, vinegar, broth, salt, and pasilla pepper into the inner pot. Add the frozen shrimp last.

4. Turn and lock the lid into place, making sure the steam-release valve is in the sealed position. Select Manual and program for 3 minutes on Low Pressure. When cooking is complete, quick release pressure manually.

5. Adjust seasoning with calamansi juice and patis. Ladle a serving into a bowl and top with ground pepper.

TIP:

For vegetarian options, omit shrimp and substitute liquid aminos for patis.

GINATAANG SITAW AT KALABASA
String Beans and Squash in Coconut Milk

Serves 4
Prep Time: 20 minutes
Active Time: 5 minutes
Pressure Cook Time: 7 minutes
Release: Quick

---

2 tbsp coconut oil

1 tbsp of garlic, minced

½ cup chopped onion

1 (1-inch piece) ginger, sliced

2 tbsp bagoong

3 cups kalabasa, chopped into 1
    to 2-inch cubes

½ lb green beans, cut into
    2-inch pieces

1 (13.5 oz) can of coconut milk

1 cup chicken broth

1 tbsp patis

½ tsp ground black pepper

1 cup baby spinach

Summers in the San Francisco Bay Area provide enough sunshine to adequately grow winter squashes like kalabasa (also known as Japanese kabocha). I should know; my parents have done it for nearly 40 years. Each fall, we harvest the squash and give them as offerings of connection to our loved ones. In this hearty dish, the pressure cooker practically pulverizes the kalabasa, creating a creamy broth akin to butternut squash soup. Include larger pieces of squash if you want to sink your teeth into them. Also, if kalabasa leaves are available in your area, they add a nice touch to this stew. *-Jeannie*

1. Preheat the Instant Pot on Sauté setting. When the inner pot is hot, pour in the coconut oil. When the oil is shimmering, add the garlic, onion, and ginger and sweat until aromatic and soft. Turn off Instant Pot.

2. Add the bagoong and sauté for 1 to 2 minutes using residual heat. Add remaining ingredients except the spinach. Stir to combine.

3. Turn and lock the lid into place, making sure the steam-release valve is in the sealed position. Select Manual and program for 7 minutes on High Pressure. When cooking is complete, quick release pressure manually.

4. Unlock and carefully remove the lid. Add baby spinach and gently stir. Cook to desired texture using residual heat.

TIPS:

Shrimp may be added for protein. We recommend sautéing ½-pound of defrosted, peeled shrimp with the aromatics in step 1, then removing the shrimp and setting them aside. Add shrimp back into the dish after the vegetables are cooked.

GISING GISING
Beans with Pork in Coconut Milk

Serves 4
Prep Time: 15 minutes
Active Time: 15 minutes
Pressure Cook Time: 0 minute
Release: Quick

---

3 tbsp cooking oil

3 cloves garlic, minced

1 medium yellow onion, minced

½ lb ground pork

2 thai chilies, minced

1 tbsp ginisang bagoong

1 (13.5 oz) can coconut milk

½ tsp salt

¼ tsp ground black pepper

1½ lb green beans, cut into
   1-inch pieces

Salt and pepper to taste

Gising gising directly translates to "wake up, wake up." That's because the spice from this dish will wake you up! Growing up, I don't recall ever eating any Filipino vegetarian dishes. There is always a little meat or bagoong thrown into any dish, even ones comprised mostly of vegetables. The main ingredients in gising gising are green beans and coconut milk, while the ground pork and bagoong are the side kicks in this dish. *-Tisha*

1. Preheat the Instant Pot on Sauté setting. When the inner pot is hot, pour in the cooking oil.

2. When the oil is shimmering, add the garlic and onion and cook for about 4 to 5 minutes until onions are translucent.

3. Add ground pork and cook for about 5 to 7 minutes until meat is no longer pink.

4. Add chilies, bagoong, coconut milk, salt, pepper, and green beans and mix well.

5. Turn and lock the lid into place, making sure the steam-release valve is in the sealed position. Select Manual and program for 0 minutes on High Pressure. When cooking is complete, quick release pressure manually.

6. Adjust seasoning with salt and pepper and serve with rice.

TIPS:

If thai chilies are not available, you can substitute with 1 tsp crushed red pepper flakes or 1 jalapeño.

If you want more control over how tender you want the green beans, you can add the green beans after step 5. Turn on Sauté Mode and add green beans and simmer for 3 to 5 minutes or until desired tenderness.

Filipino Farm-to-Table

I was born on the Pacific island of Guam after both sides of my family emigrated from the Philippines in the 1960s and '70s. From my earliest years, I have vivid memories of humid, tropical evenings, playing barefoot with my sister and cousins, as my aunts and uncles joked loudly with one another in Cebuano. During childhood, I would spend time at Lolo and Lola's house, marveling at their bountiful garden filled with talong, ampalaya, kamatis, sili, you name it. If we were making tinolang manok, Lolo would go in the yard and chop down a stalk of malunggay with his trusted bolo knife. I loved helping Lola prepare the veggies, running my fingers along the malunggay stalks, feeling their tiny green leaves pop into my little hands.

After my family moved to Northern California in 1980, I sorely missed all of those warm meals, with the freshest of homegrown gulay, especially Lola's piping hot tinolang manok and Lolo's smoky tortang talong. Luckily, my parents carried those long-held gardening traditions with us to California. Of course, due to the Mediterranean climate, we could not raise all of the varieties of fruits and vegetables that we did on the islands. Nearly 40 years later, Mom harvests upo, kalabasa, and sayote each fall to share with friends and family.

The practice of home gardening originates sa probinsya, in rural Philippines, where raising your own food is part of survival and self-sustainability for your family. I've realized that this is an art and connection to the land that our generation will lose if we don't start learning and preserving them. That's why I'm here. With these stories and these dishes, my family hopes to reclaim these roots of "farm-to-table" and cook comfort foods that remind our hearts of home.

-Jeannie

CHAPTER 9

Minatamis

Sweets

left, Puto, page 138

LECHE FLAN
Steamed Caramel Custard

Serves 10 to 12
Prep Time: 10 minutes
Active Time: 10 minutes
Pressure Cook Time: 15 minutes
Release: Quick

---

1 cup white sugar
1 (14 oz) can condensed milk
1 (12 oz) can evaporated milk
9 egg yolks
1 egg
1 tsp vanilla extract
1½ cup water

Equipment:
2 (7-inch round) metal baking pans or 2 (7-inch) llaneras (oval-shaped metal baking pans)
Aluminum foil
Instant Pot trivet

Growing up, leche flan was always a dessert my mom would make for our family parties. I remember watching her do the delicate work of separating egg yolks. She used llaneras (oval-shaped metal baking pans) inside her stove top pressure cooker to make the delicious dessert custard. This is my mom's recipe that she handed down to me. Typically, leche flan recipes call for egg yolks only, but she said that the added whole egg makes the consistency a little creamier and not as dense. *-Tisha*

1. In a small saucepan, melt sugar over low to medium heat until sugar is a golden brown color. Carefully pour caramelized sugar into the 2 round pans, making sure to evenly divide the sugar. Set aside to cool.

2. In a large mixing bowl, combine and gently mix the condensed milk, evaporated milk, egg yolks, egg, and vanilla. Divide mixture between the 2 round pans and cover each with foil.

3. Add water to the inner pot and place trivet inside. Place pan on trivet.

4. Turn and lock the lid into place, making sure the steam-release valve is in the sealed position. Select Manual and program for 15 minutes on High Pressure. When cooking is complete, quick release pressure manually.

Carefully remove the pan and repeat step 4 for the second pan. Add more water to the inner pot if necessary. Allow to cool to room temperature for approximately 1 hour. Refrigerate for 4 hours or overnight.

5. Run a butter knife along the edges of the pan to loosen the leche flan. Place serving plate on top of pan and quickly flip the flan over. Let sit for one minute before removing the pan to allow the caramelized sugar to cover the flan. Serve chilled.

CASSAVA CAKE

Serves 8 to 10
Prep Time: 10 minutes
Active Time: 10 minutes
Pressure Cook Time: 25 minutes
Release: Natural

---

1 (16 oz) package frozen
   cassava, defrosted

2 eggs

3 tbsp white sugar

¼ cup melted butter

1 cup coconut milk

¾ cup condensed milk

1 tbsp milk

Cooking oil spray

1 cup water

1 (12 oz) jar of macapuno (coconut strings) in syrup

Equipment:

Instant Pot trivet

7-inch round metal pan or
   oven-safe glass baking dish
   (7-cup capacity)

Cassava cake mainly consists of coconut milk, condensed milk and grated cassava, which is a root plant. My mom can practically whip up her famed (among my friends anyway) cassava cake with her eyes closed. So when I asked her for the recipe, it was no surprise that she gave me vague instructions like "before you add the eggs, taste it to see if it needs more sugar." While that's great advice, I went a step further and added measurements to this recipe, for your convenience! -*Tisha*

1. In a large mixing bowl, combine cassava, eggs, white sugar, butter, coconut milk, condensed milk, and milk.

2. Spray the sides of the pan with cooking oil and pour cassava mixture filling two-thirds of the way. Cover tightly with foil.

3. Add water to the inner pot and place trivet inside. Place pan on top of trivet. (Note: if you are using smaller baking pans and need to divide the mixture into two pans, you can cook them separately or try stacking them on top of each other.)

4. Turn and lock the lid into place, making sure the steam-release valve is in the sealed position. Select Manual and program for 25 minutes on High Pressure. When cooking is complete, allow pressure to release naturally. Meanwhile, preheat the broiler.

5. Unlock and carefully remove the lid. Carefully remove baking pan from inner pot.

6. Top the cassava with a thin layer of macapuno strings. Broil for 5 to 10 minutes or until brown. Be sure to keep a close watch on the cassava to prevent it from burning.

7. Let cool and serve.

BIKO
Caramelized Sticky Rice Cake

Serves 8 to 10
Prep Time: 10 minutes
Active Time: 0 minutes
Pressure Cook Time: 75 minutes
Release: Natural

---

3 cups water

1¾ cups glutinous rice, rinsed

1 (13.5 oz) can full-fat
    coconut milk

1 (13.5 oz) can coconut cream

1 tsp vanilla extract

½ cup white sugar

¼ tsp salt

Coconut caramel topping:

6 tbsp coconut cream

¼ cup brown sugar, packed

Equipment:

Instant Pot trivet

2.5 qt (10 cup) oven-safe glass
    mixing bowl that can fit inside
    the Instant Pot

Oven-safe pan, about
    9-inches square

Biko is a simple, go-to dessert or merienda (snack) sure to please everyone, including relatives, neighbors, and co-workers. Kids can even help make this dish by measuring out the ingredients and pressing the buttons on the Instant Pot. This biko has 50 to 75% less sugar than typical recipes, but trust us, it'll be plenty sweet with the caramelized coconut sauce on top. It's best served warm with a cup of coffee or tea. Bring it to a party and it will be gone in a jiffy. *-Jeannie*

1. Add water to the inner pot and place trivet inside. Place the glass bowl on top of the trivet.

2. Pour the rinsed glutinous rice into the glass bowl in the inner pot.

3. In a medium mixing bowl, combine coconut milk, coconut cream, vanilla, sugar, and salt. Mix until all the sugar is dissolved.

4. Pour the coconut milk mixture over glutinous rice in the glass bowl and stir thoroughly.

5. Turn and lock the lid into place, making sure the steam-release valve is in the sealed position. Select Manual and program for 1 hour and 15 minutes on High Pressure. When cooking is complete, release pressure naturally.

6. While rice is cooking, grease an oven-safe pan with coconut oil.

7. Preheat your conventional oven to 350 degrees.

8. In a small mixing bowl, prepare the coconut caramel topping by combining coconut cream and brown sugar. Mix until all the brown sugar is dissolved. Set aside.

9. Unlock and carefully remove the lid. With a rice paddle, gently fold in any unabsorbed coconut milk and transfer the cooked rice into the greased pan. Flatten the top of the rice "casserole" until it's evenly distributed.

Rice Jiggly Treats

Some of my most vivid childhood food memories involve pulling pillowy puto and sticky suman from my mom's large aluminum steamer. Sometimes I'd get a little too eager and singe my fingertips on the hot banana leaves.

Of our homemade Filipino sweet treats, my favorite was biko, the sticky rice cake that I always thought paired perfectly with hot cocoa, or even better, tsokolate (page 149). In elementary school, I thought biko was like a Filipino Bizarro version of the rice crispy treats my white friends would sometimes bring to class. They'd bring a tray of crackly, marshmallowy treats for everyone in celebration of a birthday or holiday. While I, the Filipino kid with the weird food, never dared to bring my beloved brown biko to share, for fear of death by embarrassment.

Oddly enough, that childhood fear is a big reason I have so much outward affection for Filipino cuisine today. I just got sick of closeting my feelings for our foods, especially our weirdly sticky, sometimes jiggly, and often rice-based sweet-treats. I love Filipino food, and my hope is that my kids will feel proud enough to say the same, without ever believing that their classmates' sweet rice squares are somehow better than ours.

-Jaymar

10. Evenly spread the coconut caramel topping on top of the rice. Place the casserole in the oven until the brown sugar begins to bubble, about 5 to 10 minutes. Switch oven to broil and place pan under broiler for about 5 minutes until caramelized and darkened to your preference.

TIPS:

We use significantly less sugar than traditional recipes. Based on what color you'd like your biko to be, you can use white or brown sugar, adding up to $1/2$ cup. I prefer the white biko "cake" base with the contrasting caramelized sauce on top.

The biko may be served with "sprinkles," such as roasted sesame seeds or a dash of sea salt.

PUTO
Steamed Cake

Serves 8 to 12
Prep Time: 15 minutes
Active Time: 0 minutes
Pressure Cook Time: 15 minutes
Release: Natural + Quick

---

1 cup all-purpose flour, sifted

⅔ cup white sugar

1 tbsp baking powder

⅛ tsp salt

⅔ cup water

1 egg white

¼ cup evaporated milk

¼ tsp vanilla extract

Melted butter, vegetable oil, or
    non-stick cooking oil spray

1½ cups water

Shredded cheddar cheese

Equipment:
Silicone egg bites molds
Aluminum foil
Instant Pot trivet

When I was little, I always enjoyed eating these little cream fluffy cupcakes called puto at our family parties. I always thought of puto as a dessert, but many people enjoy it as merienda. It's also the perfect pairing with Dinuguan (page 77),) if you're a fan. Puto can be topped with cheese or salted egg. Try adding a few drops of pandan or ube extract to the batter and you'll have a colorful display of cakes in a variety of flavors. *-Tisha*

1. In a bowl, combine flour, sugar, baking powder, and salt, and mix well with a whisk.

2. In a separate bowl, whisk water, egg white, evaporated milk, and vanilla until smooth and then add dry ingredients. Whisk until combined, getting out any lumps.

3. Lightly brush or spray silicone molds with butter or oil. Fill each mold with batter until about ³⁄₄ full. Cover lightly with foil.

4. Add water to the inner pot and place trivet inside. Place molds on top of trivet. (Note: If you're using silicone egg bite molds to cook your puto, you can stack one on top of the other in the inner pot.)

5. Turn and lock the lid into place, making sure the steam-release valve is in the sealed position. Select Manual and program for 15 minutes on Low Pressure. When cooking is complete, allow pressure to release naturally for 10 minutes, then quick release. Unlock and carefully remove the lid.

6. Remove molds and sprinkle cheese on puto. Allow to cool on counter before removing the cakes.

Repeat steps 3 to 6 until you've used all the batter. Be sure to check your pot to make sure there's ample water.

PUTONG PUTI
Steamed Rice Cake

Serves 10 to 14
Prep Time: 10 minutes
Active Time: 0 minutes
Pressure Cook Time: 20 minutes
Release: Quick

---

2 cups rice flour (do not use sweet rice flour)
¾ cup sugar
2 tsp baking powder
¼ tsp salt
1 (13.5 oz) can coconut milk
1½ cups water
Non-stick cooking spray

Equipment:
Silicone egg bites molds or ramekins
Aluminum foil
Instant Pot trivet

Here is my version of putong puti adapted for the Instant Pot. I try to cut out gluten when possible so I was pretty excited to try this recipe out. This is definitely not the fluffy white puto I'm used to as this puto is chewier and more dense. It reminds me of Japanese mochi actually. It's a simple recipe and only requires five ingredients. And if you want to make them with different flavors, try adding 1 to 2 ts of ube or pandan extract. It will definitely add lots of color to your dessert presentation. *-Tisha*

1. In a large bowl, combine the flour, sugar, baking powder, salt, coconut milk and mix well with a whisk.

2. Spray silicone molds or ramekins with non-stick cooking spray. Fill molds about ¾ of the way with mixture and then cover with foil.

3. Add water to the inner pot and place trivet inside. Place molds on top of the trivet.

4. Turn and lock the lid into place, making sure the steam-release valve is in the sealed position. Select Manual and program for 20 minutes on High Pressure.

5. When cooking is complete, quick release pressure manually. Unlock and carefully remove the lid and the molds. Allow to cool on counter before removing the cakes.

TIP:

If you are using silicone egg bite molds, you can also stack two of them in your Instant Pot while steaming.

KUTSINTA
Golden Rice Cake

Serves 6 to 8
Prep Time: 10 minutes
Active Time: 0 minutes
Pressure Cook Time: 25 minutes
Release: Quick

---

1 tsp annatto powder

3 tbsp water

½ cup all-purpose flour

½ cup tapioca flour

¾ cup brown sugar

2 tsp lye water

1½ cup water

Grated coconut

Equipment:

Silicone egg molds

Aluminum foil

Instant Pot trivet

Kutsin-TA. I was corrected by my uncle when I brought some over for a family party. He and my dad approved of my kutsinta, but I just needed to work on putting the emphasis on the "TA" when pronouncing it. Although my Tagalog pronunciation needs some work, I was quite proud of myself when I figured out how to make kutsinta in the Instant Pot. This is a very easy recipe to make using silicone egg molds. You can find these ingredients at Asian markets. But if you don't have one nearby, they're also available on Amazon. *-Tisha*

1. In a small bowl, mix annatto powder and water and set aside.

2. In a large mixing bowl, combine all-purpose flour, tapioca flour, and brown sugar. Add lye water and mix using a whisk. Add annatto mixture and mix.

3. Spray silicone egg molds with non-stick cooking spray and fill molds about halfway to two thirds of the way. Cover molds with foil.

4. Add water to the inner pot and place trivet inside. Place molds on top of trivet.

5. Turn and lock the lid into place, making sure the steam-release valve is in the sealed position. Select Manual and program for 25 minutes on High Pressure. When cooking is complete, quick release pressure manually.

6. Carefully remove molds and allow to cool for 30 minutes. With a small spoon, gently run spoon under to remove from molds.

7. Serve with grated coconut.

GINATAANG MAIS
Sweet Corn Porridge

Serves 4
Prep Time: 5 minutes
Active Time: 2 minutes
Pressure Cook Time: 3 minutes
Release: Natural + Quick

---

2 cups water

1 (15 oz) can whole kernel corn
    with liquid

¾ cup glutinous rice

1 (14 oz) can coconut milk

¼ cup white sugar

Sea salt

Toppings (optional):

Mango

Toasted shredded coconut

Toasted rice crispies

Brown sugar

Condensed milk

Chia seeds

Sesame seeds

Sliced almonds

Ginataang mais can be served as a snack or as a dessert. It's a simple, sweet rice porridge suffused with coconut milk and corn. Like Ginataang Bilo-Bilo (page 144), this dish can be served hot or cold, though my tummy has always enjoyed it warm. Depending on your preference, you can use fresh, frozen, canned, or roasted corn. Also, you can play around with different types of rice or toppings. *-Jeannie*

1. In the inner pot, add water and corn with liquid.

2. In a small strainer, rinse the rice under the kitchen faucet. Do not soak the rice.

3. Add the rice immediately to inner pot. Stir gently until all ingredients are combined.

4. Turn and lock the lid into place, making sure the steam-release valve is in sealed position. Select Manual and program for 3 minutes on High Pressure and turn off Keep Warm setting. When cooking is complete, release pressure naturally for 10 minutes then quick release the remaining pressure manually.

5. Unlock and carefully remove the lid. Add coconut milk and sugar. Select Sauté and stir constantly for 2 minutes as porridge thickens. Turn off Instant Pot.

6. Serve in small bowls and add toppings as you desire. Sprinkle with sea salt to taste.

TIPS:

You may grill 2 to 3 cobs of corn or use a torch to char the kernels. Carefully cut the kernels off the cob and add in step 1 along with 2/3 cup water. The corn will cook thoroughly in the Instant Pot, so there's no need to fully cook it on the grill. The charred kernels will add a roasted flavor to the dish.

We cut the sugar amount from what is normally found in traditional recipes, but you can add more sugar to your taste.

GINATAANG BILO-BILO

Glutinous Rice Balls in Coconut Milk

Serves 10
Prep Time: 30 minutes
Active Time: 5 minutes
Pressure Cook Time: 1 minute
Release: Intermittent (see tips)

---

2 cups glutinous rice flour

1 cup cold water

½ (20 oz) can yellow jackfruit
   in syrup

2 (13.5 oz) cans coconut milk

1½ cup water

¼ cup white sugar

1 medium sweet potato, cut into
   1-inch cubes

1 medium ube, cut into
   1-inch cubes

3 medium just ripe saba bananas

½ cup small sago pearls

Sea salt to taste (optional)

Ginataang bilo-bilo is essentially a dessert stew, full of starchy, sweet, and chewy goodness. The dish's name derives from bilog, meaning "round," pointing to the signature glutinous rice balls that define this sweet concoction. If you love Taiwanese boba, you probably love bilo-bilo; though this dessert cannot and should not be eaten with a fat straw. It must be savored by the spoonful, bite by delicate bite. Bilo-bilo can be served cold or warm. I prefer it warm, as the heat heightens the flavors of the root vegetables, tanginess of the langka, and the mochi-gumminess of the rice balls. Beware—it's nearly impossible to eat just one serving. -Jeannie

Prepare the rice balls:

1. In a medium mixing bowl, add the glutinous rice flour, then cold water. Mix until water is fully absorbed. With your hands, manipulate mixture until a stiff dough forms.

2. Roll ½-inch dough balls and place on a tray an inch apart. Cover the tray with plastic wrap to keep the balls from drying out; set aside until ready to cook.

Prepare the sweet stew:

3. Cut the jackfruit into strips and reserve 1 cup of the jackfruit syrup from the can.

4. Place the jackfruit, jackfruit syrup, coconut milk, water, sugar, sweet potato, ube, and banana in the inner pot. Stir until combined.

5. Scatter the sago pearls throughout the pot so they don't all fall in one clump.

6. Turn and lock the lid into place, making sure the steam-release valve is in the sealed position. Select Manual and program for 1 minute on High Pressure.

7. When cooking is complete, turn off Instant Pot. Carefully release pressure intermittently. See tips for more.

8. Unlock and carefully remove the lid. Select Sauté. Place the rice balls one by one around the pot, so they are less likely to stick together. Boil the balls until they float to the top, indicating that they are cooked. Turn off Instant Pot.

9. Carefully remove inner pot and let cool for 10 to 15 minutes before serving. The ginataan will thicken as it cools.

TIPS:

'Intermittent' pressure release means to carefully switch the steam release handle from 'Sealing' position to 'Venting' position every 2 or 3 seconds until the float valve drops down.

You can dye the rice balls with food coloring. Trendy bilo-bilo colors are pink, green, or purple. I prefer purple as a nod to ube. Add food coloring to cold water in step 1, before combining with rice flour

We use significantly less sugar than traditional recipes. You may sweeten to your taste.

For low-carb or diabetic diets, try sugar substitutes like stevia or allulose.

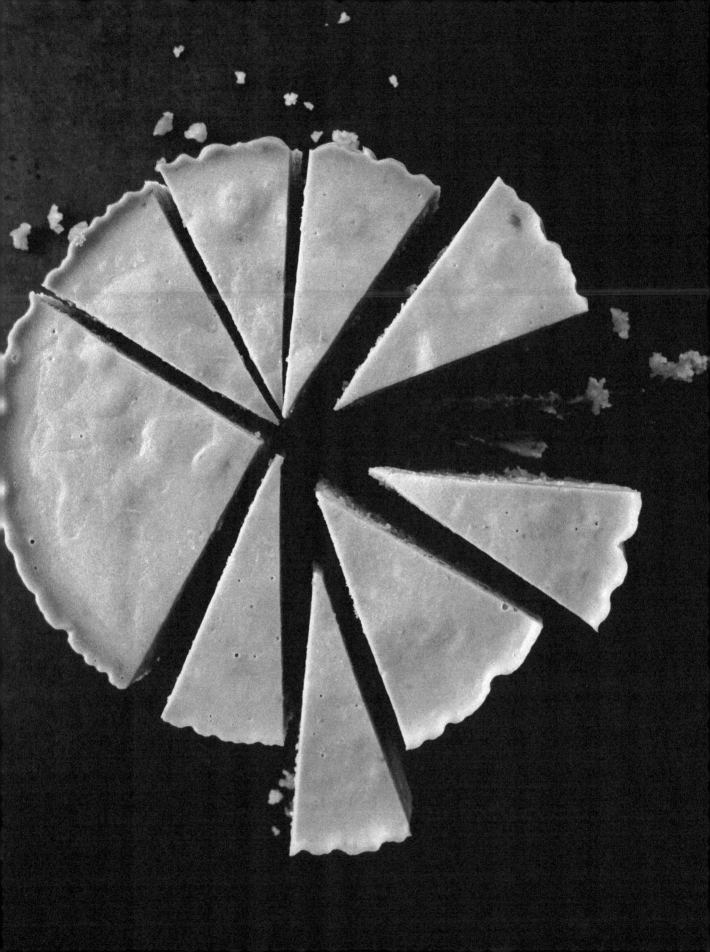

UBE CHEESECAKE

Serves 6 to 8
Prep Time: 15 minutes
Active Time: 0 minutes
Pressure Cook Time: 15 minutes
Release: Natural

For the cake:

2 (8 oz) packages cream cheese

¼ cup sour cream

⅓ cup white sugar

¾ cup ube halaya (purple
   yam jam)

3 tsp ube extract

3 eggs, room temperature

1½ cups water

For the crust:

1 packet graham crackers

2 tbsp white sugar

4 tbsp butter, melted

Equipment:

Food processor

Parchment paper

7-inch springform pan

Hand mixer

Instant Pot trivet

Heavy-duty aluminum foil

Not to be mistaken for taro, ube has been a longtime staple in Filipino desserts and has recently made its way into mainstream American culture. This yam adds a sweet and nutty flavor to desserts and is easy to identify by its deep purple color, making ube desserts very Instagram-worthy. In this recipe, I used ube halaya (purple yam jam) and ube extract to make ube cheesecake. Cheesecake is probably one of the most popular desserts to make in the Instant Pot because you can cut your cooking time in half. *-Tisha*

1. About 30 to 60 minutes in advance, take cream cheese, sour cream, and eggs out of the refrigerator so they can come to room temperature.

Prepare the crust:

2. Break graham crackers into food processor and pulse until fine. Alternatively, you can put the graham crackers in a resealable plastic bag and crush the crackers into crumbs using a rolling pin.

3. In a small bowl, combine 1 cup graham cracker crumbs, 2 tbsp sugar, and butter. Place a larger circle of parchment paper on the bottom of a 7-inch springform pan. Spray the liner with cooking oil and pour crumb mixture into pan and press evenly to form the crust.

Make the cake:

4. In a large mixing bowl, combine cream cheese, sour cream, ⅓ cup sugar, ube halaya, and ube extract using a hand mixer at low speed. Add eggs one at a time and continue mixing at low speed until all ingredients are fully incorporated. Be careful not to overmix batter.

5. Spray the sides of the pan with cooking oil. Pour batter into springform pan and tap pan on counter to get air bubbles out.

recipe continues >

UBE CHEESECAKE

continued >

6. Add water to the inner pot and place trivet inside.

7. Make a sling using an 18-inch piece of heavy-duty aluminum foil and fold it into thirds lengthwise and place the springform on the center. Carefully lower the spring-form onto the trivet using the sling. Fold down the excess foil from the sling to ensure that the pot closes properly.

8. Turn and lock the lid into place, making sure the steam-release valve is in the sealed position. Select Manual and program for 15 minutes on High Pressure. When cooking is complete, allow pressure to release naturally.

9. Unlock and carefully remove the lid. Remove the cheesecake using foil sling and place on a wire rack to cool. Gently blot any water on the cheesecake with a paper towel.

10. Cover and refrigerate for 4 hours or overnight.

11. To remove the cheesecake from the pan, run a thin knife around the inside of the pan and release the spring to remove the round pan rim.

TSOKOLATE
Native Hot Chocolate

Serves 6
Prep Time: 0 minutes
Active Time: 10 minutes
Pressure Cook Time: n/a
Release: n/a

---

6 cups water
6 to 12 blocks of tablea
Milk (optional)
Sugar (optional)

My mom brought me tablea from her last trip to the Philippines so I could make tsokolate for my kids. Tsokolate is very rich in flavor and has a thicker consistency than your average American hot chocolate. Tablea is made from dried roasted cacao beans that are ground, often with sugar added prior to being shaped. Typically, they come in tablets (hence the name), but the ones she brought me were ball-shaped. I recently learned that a lot of tablea originates in my dad's home province of Batangas, which is said to produce some of the best in the Philippines. However, if you have a Filipino market nearby, you don't have to travel far to get your tablea. Alternatively, if you like cinnamon, you can try Mexican hot chocolate which is available at your local Latin American market. -Tisha

1. Add water to the inner pot and preheat the Instant Pot on Sauté setting.

2. Add tablea and whisk until tablea dissolve completely. Turn off Instant Pot.

3. Add milk and sugar to taste.

MANGO ROYALE CHEESECAKE

Serves 6 to 8
Prep Time: 25 minutes
Active Time: 0 minutes
Pressure Cook Time: 15 minutes
Release: Natural

For the cake:

2 (8 oz) packages cream cheese

¼ cup sour cream (optional)

3 eggs

½ cup white sugar

6 tbsp Manila mangoes, freshly pureed

1 tsp vanilla extract

1 cup water

For the crust:

1 packet graham crackers

2 tbsp white sugar

4 tbsp butter, melted

Equipment:

Food processor

Parchment paper

Non-stick cooking oil spray

7-inch springform pan

Hand mixer

Heavy-duty aluminum foil

This dessert is a mango-flavored cheesecake with a simple Filipino Mango Royale topping. I was first introduced to Mango Royale in the Philippines by Tita Dely, a matriarch of my friend's family. Tita Dely's Mango Royale had layers of crushed graham crackers, sweetened cream, and fresh mango slices, all frozen into an icebox cake. Given the decadence of this cheesecake, only one layer of Mango Float topping is added as a tangy pairing. *-Jeannie*

Follow steps 1 to 3 for Ube Cheesecake on page 147.

Make the cake:

4. In a large mixing bowl, combine cream cheese, sour cream, and ½ cup sugar using a hand mixer at low speed. Add eggs one at a time and then add mango puree and vanilla. Mix at low speed until all ingredients are fully incorporated, being careful not to overmix batter.

5. Spray the sides of the pan with cooking oil. Pour batter into springform pan and tap pan on counter to get air bubbles out.

6. Add water to the inner pot and place trivet inside.

7. Make a sling using an 18-inch piece of heavy-duty aluminum foil and fold it into thirds lengthwise and place the springform on the center. Carefully lower the springform onto the trivet using the sling. Fold down the excess foil from the sling to ensure that the pot closes properly.

8. Turn and lock the lid into place, making sure the steam-release valve is in the sealed position. Select Manual and program for 15 minutes on High Pressure. When cooking is complete, allow pressure to release naturally.

9. Unlock and carefully remove the lid. Remove the cheesecake using foil sling and place on a wire rack to cool. Gently blot any water on the cheesecake with a paper towel.

10. Cover and refrigerate for 4 hours or overnight.

Mango Royale topping:

2 Manila mangoes, peeled and pureed

1 tsp calamansi juice

1 tsp sugar

1 tsp vanilla extract

1 cup organic whipping cream

11. While the cheesecake is chilling, put a medium-sized mixing bowl in the freezer. You will use this to make your fresh whipped cream.

Prepare the Mango Royale topping:

12. In a small mixing bowl, combine mange puree with calamansi juice and set aside.

13. Remove your ice-cold mixing bowl from the freezer. Place whipping cream, sugar, and vanilla extract in mixing bowl. Mix with hand mixer until stiff peaks form.

14. Remove the cheesecake from the refrigerator. Gently blot any excess water with a paper towel.

15. Coat the top of the cheesecake with whipped cream, then add a layer of mango puree on top of whipped cream. Top with $1/2$ cup crushed graham crackers.

Remove the cheesecake from the pan:

16. Run a thin plastic knife around the inside of the pan and release the spring to remove the rim.

17. If the sides of your cheesecake look a bit uneven, you may use the leftover whipped cream to frost the sides of your cake.

CALAMANSI CURD

Serves 12
Prep Time: 10 minutes
Active Time: 0 minutes
Pressure Cook Time: 10 minutes
Release: Natural + Quick

---

6 tbsp butter, at room
   temperature
1 cup white sugar
3 large eggs
2 large egg yolks
¾ cup calamansi juice (from
   about 20 to 30 calamansi)
1 tbsp grated calamansi zest
1½ cups water

Equipment:
Mason jar or oven-safe glass dish
Hand mixer
Instant Pot trivet

Calamansi is known for being rich in vitamin C and antioxidants. I've been wanting to make lemon curd in my Instant Pot for awhile. And since my mom's calamansi tree had an abundance of fruit, I thought I would try making calamansi curd instead. If you're not familiar with the calamansi fruit, it is a small round citrus that's orange when fully ripe, and sometimes confused with kumquats. Calamansi is often harvested and used while still green. It can be found in many Asian markets, but if you don't have one nearby, you can substitute lemons for this recipe. This curd can be used in making cheesecake and as a topping on ice cream or plain yogurt. It's also delicious on toast, waffles, pancakes or pandesal! -Tisha

1. In a large mixing bowl, use a hand mixer on medium speed. Cream butter and sugar for about 2 minutes.

2. Add eggs and egg yolks, one at a time, mixing until combined. Then add calamansi juice and mix for 1 minute. Mixture may look a little curdled, but that's normal.

3. Pour mixture into a large mason jar or an oven-safe glass dish that will fit inside the inner cooking pot and cover with foil. Add water to the inner pot and place trivet inside. Place your mason jar or glass dish on the trivet.

4. Turn and lock the lid into place, making sure the steam-release valve is in the sealed position. Select Manual and program for 10 minutes on High Pressure. When cooking is complete, allow pressure to release naturally for 10 minutes.

5. Unlock and carefully remove the lid. Remove the glass dish or mason jar using oven-safe gloves.

6. Allow calamansi curd to cool for 30 minutes. It will thicken as it starts to cool down. Add calamansi zest and stir.

7. Cool and serve or store in refrigerator.

CHAPTER 10
Sari-Sari
Miscellaneous

left, Nilagang Mani, page 162

BANANA KETCHUP

Yields 1 cup
Prep Time: 5 minutes
Active Time: 12 minutes
Pressure Cook Time: n/a
Release: n/a

¼ ripe banana (not saba)
1 (8 oz) can tomato sauce
½ tbsp white vinegar
1 tbsp white sugar
¼ tsp garlic powder
⅛ tsp salt

Equipment:
Handheld immersion blender

Under the harsh and uncertain conditions of World War II in the Philippines, saba (native bananas) became a common replacement for tomatoes. This eventually led to the creation of a staple sauce we now call "banana ketchup." This sweet, tangy condiment goes well with fried chicken, lumpiang shanghai, and sweet potato fries as well as with breakfast dishes such as scrambled eggs or your favorite silog (rice, eggs, and meat). Banana ketchup is also an essential ingredient in Filipino Spaghetti (page 37), giving its signature sweetness. What sets this ketchup apart from the store-bought version is this recipe uses tomatoes and absolutely no artificial coloring! *-Jeannie*

1. In a medium bowl, mash the banana using a fork until it reaches a lumpy consistency. You should have about 2 tbsp of mashed banana.

2. Add all other ingredients and blend with a handheld immersion blender. Make sure that your vessel has high enough walls to avoid any splatter.

3. Transfer mixture to a small saucepan. On medium heat, bring the mixture to a soft boil, then reduce to low heat and simmer for 10 minutes, stirring often to avoid burning and splattery bubbles.

4. Let cool completely and store in a glass container or jar.

SALABAT
Fresh Ginger Tea

Serves 6
Prep Time: 5 minutes
Active Time: 3 minutes
Pressure Cook Time: 2 minutes
Release: Natural

---

6 cups water
1 (3-inch piece) fresh ginger, sliced
Honey to taste
6 calamansi, halved (or 1 lemon, sliced)

Anytime I feel the onset of a cold, cough, or sore throat, I turn to salabat. This simple recipe is an all-natural remedy, with the key ingredient being ginger, a super-food full of antioxidants. It can improve digestion and immunity, soothe an upset stomach, and reduce inflammation. But you certainly don't need to have a cold to enjoy the benefits of a hot cup of comforting salabat. *-Tisha*

1. Add water and ginger to the inner pot.

2. Turn and lock the lid into place, making sure the steam-release valve is in the sealed position. Select Manual and program for 2 minutes on High Pressure. When cooking is complete, allow pressure to release naturally.

3. Strain with a fine-mesh sieve and serve with honey and calamansi to taste.

TIPS:

Storage: leftover tea can be cooled and stored in the refrigerator for up to one week. You can reheat it or drink chilled.

If you have any leftover ginger, peel and thinly slice it then store in the freezer for the next time you want to make salabat!

SARSA NG LECHON
Sweet Pork Liver Sauce

Yields 1½ cups
Prep Time: 5 minutes
Active Time: 10 minutes
Pressure Cook Time: 1 minute
Release: Quick

½ lb fresh pork liver

½ to 1 cup milk

2 cups + 2 tbsp water, divided

2 tsp cornstarch

2 tbsp cooking oil

1½ tbsp garlic, minced

⅓ cup minced yellow onion

¼ tsp salt

½ tsp ground black pepper

¼ cup white vinegar

⅛ cup brown sugar

2 tsp dark soy sauce

⅓ cup unseasoned bread crumbs

Equipment:
Instant Pot trivet
Immersion blender

For my Lola's 70th birthday in Cebu, we celebrated with a traditional lechon. I remember giggling as I watched my younger cousin Ryan bite into the roasted pig's snout covered in lechon sauce. "Mmm! This is good!" he exclaimed. Sarsa ng lechon is essential for serving roasted pig or for making paksiw na lechon. It is traditionally made with liver (pork or chicken), but people commonly just buy a bottle of Mang Tomas for convenience. Surprisingly, the store-bought lechon sauce contains no liver, so it lacks the highly nutritious vitamins B-12 and A, folate, copper, riboflavin, iron, and choline. Try this recipe and get your sauce on! -*Jeannie*

Prepare the liver:

1. Rinse the liver. In a resealable bag, place liver and pour in enough milk to fully cover the liver. Seal the bag and put in fridge for at least one hour.

2. Remove liver from milk bath and pat dry with a paper towel. Slice into pieces about 1-inch thick.

3. Add 1 cup water to the inner pot and place trivet inside. Place liver on trivet. Turn and lock the lid into place, making sure the steam-release valve is in the sealed position. Select Manual and program for 1 minute on High Pressure. When cooking is complete, quick release pressure manually. Remove the liver and set aside to cool.

4. Remove water and trivet from the inner pot. Dry the inside of the inner pot and return it to Instant Pot base.

Prepare the sauce:

5. In a small bowl, add cornstarch and 2 tbsp cold water, stirring well until cornstarch dissolves. Set aside.

6. Preheat the Instant Pot on Sauté setting. When the inner pot is hot, pour in the cooking oil. When the oil is shim-

mering, add the garlic and onion and sweat until aromatic and soft. Turn off Instant Pot.

7. Add liver pieces, 1 cup water, salt, pepper, vinegar, brown sugar, soy sauce, and bread crumbs. With a handheld immersion blender, blend the sauce until all the liver is completely processed. Sauce will be runny like a soup.

8. Select Sauté and adjust to Less mode. Once sauce is boiling softly, slowly add cornstarch mixture, stirring constantly with a whisk until fully integrated. Continue boiling until sauce sticks to the back of a spoon, having the thickness of turkey gravy.

9. Serve warm. Any remaining sauce can be stored in a glass container in the refrigerator.

TIP:

Chicken liver can be substituted for pork liver, depending on your preference.

NILAGANG MANI
Boiled Peanuts

Serves 4
Prep Time: 5 minutes
Active Time: 2 minutes
Pressure Cook Time: 80 minutes
Release: Natural + Quick

---

1 lb raw peanuts, washed
4 ½ tbsp coarse sea salt
Water

Equipment:
Instant Pot trivet

The trendy term "street food" has become way overused in the marketing of ethnic fast food and appetizers lately. (For example, there's nothing "street" about the street fare lettuce wraps at PF Chang's.) Boiled peanuts, by contrast, are the opposite of trendy; they're just delicious. And they are great to snack on with a cold San Miguel beer or inside your car while crawling through Manila traffic. *-Art*

1. Add peanuts, salt, and enough water to cover peanuts and make them float.

2. Place trivet on top of the peanuts. Weigh the trivet down with a heavy, oven-safe bowl full of water to submerge the peanuts.

3. Turn and lock the lid into place, making sure the steam-release valve is in the sealed position. Select Manual and program for 1 hour and 20 minutes on High Pressure. When cooking is complete, allow pressure to release naturally for 10 minutes and then quick release remaining pressure.

TIP:

For firmer peanuts, program for 55 minutes instead, with 10 minutes for natural release plus and quick release. For extra soft peanuts, set to 100 minutes, and natural release for.

ITLOG NA MAALAT AT KAMATIS
Salted Egg and Tomato Salad

Serves 2
Prep Time: 35 minutes
Active Time: 15 minutes
Pressure Cook Time: 5 minutes
Release: Quick

For salted eggs:
1 dozen eggs (chicken or duck)
6 cups water, divided
1 cup salt

For salad:
4 medium tomatoes, chopped
1 small daikon, chopped
2 tbsp chopped onion leaves
½ tbsp cilantro, minced
Juice of 4 calamansi
⅛ tsp sugar
¼ tsp ground black pepper

Equipment:
Instant Pot trivet

Salted egg, tomato salad, and hot rice is the easiest way to feed an unexpected guest when the options in the kitchen are slim. I've been that unexpected guest many times, and eating a few servings of this dish always made me feel at home. Make sure you enjoy it kamayan-style (using just your hands to eat) to elevate the textures and flavors. This dish pairs wonderfully with fried dried fish, like dilis or tuyo. *-Art*

Cure the eggs in salt:

1. Add 5 cups water and salt to a storable container and stir until salt dissolves. Add eggs and soak for **3 weeks** in the refrigerator. You may create a calendar reminder to help you remember to take them out of the salt bath on the correct date.

Cook the salted eggs:

2. After eggs have fully cured, remove them from salt bath. Add 1 cup water to the inner pot and place trivet inside. Place the eggs on trivet. Turn and lock the lid into place, making sure the steam-release valve is in the sealed position. Select Manual and program for 5 minutes on High Pressure. When cooking is complete, quick release pressure manually.

3. Mark each egg and store them in the refrigerator.

Make the salad:

4. Coarsely chop two of the salted eggs.

5. In a medium-sized bowl, add all ingredients together and mix well. Lemon can be substituted for calamansi.

COOKING TIME CHARTS

Meat and Seafood	Cooking Time (minutes)
Beef, oxtail	40-50
Beef, ribs	20-25
Beef, shank	25-30
Chicken, breast	6-8
Chicken, cut with bones	10-14
Chicken (frozen)	15-18
Fish, whole	4-7
Fish, fillet	2-4
Fish, steak	3-6
Pork, belly (cubes)	15-20
Pork, belly (strips)	12-15
Pork, butt or shoulder (cubes)	15-20
Pork, ribs	15-20
Shrimp or prawn	0-4
Squid	0-4

Vegetables, Rice, Beans, and Other Ingredients	Cooking Time (minutes)
Ampalaya (bitter melon)	0-3
Bok Choy	2-5
Broccoli	0
Cauliflower	0-2
Eggplant (slices or chunks)	2-4
Kalabasa (squash)	4-7
Kangkong (water spinach)	1 min (sauté)
Monggo (mung bean)	10-12
Potatoes (cubed)	3-5
Rice, brown	20-22
Rice, jasmine	4
Rice, white	4
Sitaw (string bean)	3-5
Spinach	0-1 (sauté)
Upo (bottle gourd)	0-4

RECIPE INDEX

Disclaimer: While this index is intended to serve as a helpful guideline, we cannot 100% guarantee the finished dishes will satisfy the listed dietary preferences, as packaged ingredients may vary. If you have any allergies, please double-check all of your ingredients.

Vegetarian

Weeknight Dinner

ACKNOWLEDGMENTS

From All of Us

Maraming salamat sa aming mga
Eksperto ng pagluluto: mga magulang, lolo, at lola
Galing sa puso ang itong libro.

Tisha Gonda Domingo

Special thanks to my mom who has instilled in me a love for cooking at a young age, my mother-in-law who continues to share her vast knowledge of family recipes, and my friends and family (especially my dad) who have tasted my recipes and supported us through this amazing journey of learning and discovery. And of course, to Jorell, thank you for searching Facebook for a Filipino Instant Pot page and taking this leap of faith in creating this group. None of this would be possible without you!

Jorell Domingo

Thank you all the family that has collectively shaped my love for Filipino food. To my Mom and Dad, whose cooking still makes me feel the comfort and love of my childhood; my lolas, especially Grandma Cora, who helped raise me and passed her love on through cooking; my sister, mother-in-law, titas/titos, and cousins, whose cooking has always challenged my waistline. To the friends who supported us throughout this journey, especially those Bruins who showed me that Filipino culture can be shared through music, dancing, teaching, writing, political activism, entrepreneurship, and food. To the Filipino IP Community—you inspire me with your creativity and desire to learn and share. To my kids, who I hope will continue to learn about and love Filipino food. Finally to Tisha, who urged me to start the group on Facebook and embraced the opportunity to collaborate on this project. You amaze me every day.

Jeannie E. Celestial

I honor and appreciate my grandparents: Francisco, Simpleciana, Apolonio, and Petrona and those who inspired my recipes: Mom, Dad, Mama Mel, Ate Mellie, Leila, Ella de Castro Baron, Adelina Tancioco, and Titas Corazon, Julita, Elvira and Dely. Thank you to the islands that give me breath: the Philippines, Guam, Hawaii, and the Bay Area. My contributions to this book would not have been possible without my partner Art and our joy, MJ.

Art Swenson

Thanks to my lola who taught me that patient and loving craft transforms cooking into wizardry. Thanks to my mom who taught me to trust all of my senses while cooking to decide when enough is enough. Thanks to my tito Eddie who taught me that men could be great cooks. Thanks to my wife, Jeannie, who helped me overcome my imposter syndrome as a Filipino cook.

Jaymar Cabebe

To Mom and Dad, you never gave up on me, and now look—I eat monggo, ampalaya, and all kinds of seafood! To my lolas and lolos, thank you for inspiring me to know my roots and to make sure my son knows his too. And finally, to Dianne. Without you, I do not cook; I do not write; I do not live. Love to you all.

Romeo Roque-Nido

Mad props to the the turo-turos, and small mom-and-pop shops. For decades you have been champions of our food, offering it proudly unaltered for the community. Robert "Ka Enteng" Dacquel, you were unapologetically yourself, hawking adobo, pancit, and lumpia from a street food cart in the 1980s and into the 2000s. You were a precursor to food revolutions and movements. And finally, Nowie, thanks for believing in me and encouraging me to pursue my passions. Even as I worked during vacations and missed family parties, you pushed me to keep on keeping on. Salamat.

Pssssst!

 FilipinoInstantPotCookbook

 Groups/FilipinoInstantPotRecipes

ABOUT THE AUTHORS

Tisha Gonda Domingo

Tisha was born and raised in Southern California, where she currently resides with her family. Aside from a two-year gig as an English teacher in Japan, Tisha has spent the majority of her career working in publicity at a major film and television studio. She loves spending time outdoors, traveling, trying new foods, and cooking. She finds great joy in cooking for the family, especially when she gets a stamp of approval from her kids and husband Jorell. Being a part of the Filipino Instant Pot Community on Facebook has inspired her to expand her Filipino recipe repertoire, and she is excited to pass these recipes on to her two young kids.

Jorell Domingo

Jorell was born on Guam and spent most of his formative years growing up on a military base just outside of Tokyo, Japan. He then moved to California to attend UCLA, where he met his wife Tisha (Go Bruins!). Jorell spends much of his free time with his family (kids'/school/outdoor activities), snowboarding, supporting his Bruins, Lakers, Dodgers and Kings, plane spotting, reading, and exploring local sites/eats. While his favorite dishes are his mom's mechado and nilaga, Japanese food also provides a similar sense of comfort and joy. And he, along with his wife, started the ever-growing Filipino Instant Pot Community group on Facebook.

Jeannie E. Celestial, Ph.D

Jeannie was born on Guam to Visayan and Tagalog families and grew up in Vallejo, California. Her consciousness was raised at UC Berkeley where she became a scholar-activist, surrounded by committed Filipinx siblings, fostering social change. Now a licensed clinical psychologist, she facilitates the healing of hearts and minds and works to destigmatize mental health concerns. Home cooking with the Instant Pot is one way Jeannie bridges connection with her ancestors, modern family life, and future generations. She aspires to become fluent in Tagalog and good food--one of the primary Filipino love languages.

Art Swenson

Art's Caucasian dad grew up eating peanut butter and jelly sandwiches, while his Pinay mom grew up eating kare-kare and bagoong. These facts depressed him as a child because of his very itchy peanut allergy. At the age of 25, he decided to carefully eat only the chocolate from a Snickers bar. (After a nibble or two, he gobbled up the whole thing, peanuts and all, because all he really wanted was to eat a friggin' Snickers bar, goddamnit!) To his shock, only pleasure erupted; his allergy was gone, and Snickers bars were thoroughly awesome. Years of peanut enjoyment later, Art fully embraces kare-kare and bagoong over peanut butter and jelly.

Romeo Roque-Nido

Romeo is a San Francisco Bay Area native. His interests include classic Italian bicycles and finding appropriate headphones for particular life situations. Occasionally, he binges on Tagalog movies and music. Romeo stays busy by having fun with his lovely wife and their two young kids. His lola once told him, while teaching him to cook, "one needs to cook to survive," to which he replied, "but one also needs to eat, in order to live." That internal conflict of having to survive versus wanting to live, has him at a corporate job while dreaming of operating his own food establishment one day.

Jaymar Cabebe

Born and raised in Southern California, Jaymar currently lives in the Bay Area where he spends his days as an operations consultant, helping start-ups start up. His favorite Filipino food memories include his lola rolling Mochiko flour into little balls for ginataan and his uncle bringing a straight-up whole goat to his graduation party. Jaymar's non-food-related loves include basketball, martial arts, and most of all, his wife Dianne and their toddler-baby. His parents speak Waray, Ilocano, Pangasinan, and Tagalog, while Jaymar, regrettably, only speaks English.

CPSIA information can be obtained
at www.ICGtesting.com
Printed in the USA
LVHW011625121120
671500LV00007B/280